Islam and Democracy

By Dr. Anab Whitehouse

Table of Contents

4

1) Islam and Democracy

According to Imam Rauf:

"America is substantively an 'Islamic' country by which I mean a country whose systems remarkably embody the principles that Islamic law requires of a government." (p. 80 of: *What's Right With Islam).*

In saying such things, I believe that Imam Rauf fails to understand the basic form of the American approach to constitutional democracy, as well as, oddly enough, seems to fail to understand some very important principles within Islam.

First of all, despite the modern clamor among some Muslims concerning the need to create an Islamic state, and in spite of the centuries of writings across a variety of Muslim theologians concerning the idea of Islamic governance, there really is no such thing as Islamic law – that is, there is no such thing as a body of Islamic doctrines and principles that forms a legal system that should be imposed on other people.

There is such a thing as Muslim law that is based on various hermeneutical systems that have been developed in conjunction with what some Muslims have taken Islam to be. However, Muslim law really often has very little to do with the actual nature of Islam.

What Islam requires from government is that those who govern should behave in accordance with the requirements of Islam as a personal path focused on realizing the character of truth and reality in relation to one's own life. In other words, the relation of Islam to governance is entirely a matter of rulers and leaders complying with the principles of Islam in relation to their own: character, integrity, judiciousness, honesty, benevolence, fairness, modesty, impartiality, tolerance, reasonableness without private passions, virtue, capacity to demonstrate high-mindedness with respect to the public good, and their willingness to sacrifice their own interests for the sake of others, so that those leaders serve truth, justice, and the people in all matters.

Consequently, there is nothing in such governance that is to be required of anyone except the leaders. When leaders act in accordance with truth, justice, and principles of personal character, one has Islamic governance. When leaders seek to act in accordance with other than truth, justice, or principles of personal character, then one does not have Islamic governance.

There is no system of law to be applied to, or imposed on, the people. The principles that are to be applied should all be directed toward the leaders.

John F. Kennedy once said in his inaugural address:

"Ask not what your country can do for you – ask what you can do for your country."

The words were addressed to his listeners, but they should have been directed only toward him and other members of his government … or any other government.

The duty of a leader is to serve truth, justice, and the people. The duty of a leader is not to expect that others should serve his or her philosophy or agenda.

The term that the Framers of the Constitution used in this respect is: republican government. The principle was of such central importance to the Framers that they institutionalized it in Article IV, Section 4 of the Constitution -- a facet of the Constitution that placed the federal government under an obligation to guarantee each of the states of the union the values and principles inherent in such republican government.

Republican government has nothing to do with the philosophy of the Republican Party. In fact, much of the time, the parties of both the Republicans and Democrats are decidedly anti-republican in character.

Republican government encompasses a set of principles and values that are to be followed by the leaders rather than imposed on the citizens of the respective states. Republican government required leaders to be: benevolent, virtuous, impartial, reasonable, honorable, unbiased, honest, egalitarian, impartial, judicious, tolerant, as well as required them to give expression to character and integrity through all of their behaviors.

If a government cannot act in accordance with republican principles and values, then the constitutional document that supposedly provides the raison d'être for governance, really starts at no beginning and works toward no end. There is no real democracy except within a framework of "leaders" who operate out of a republican perspective. A constitution that is not embedded in the readiness of leaders of the executive, the legislature, and the judiciary to behave in a republican manner is an empty exercise of form, without anything of substantive value.

Many people have remarked how the Constitution of the old Soviet Union was a wonderful-sounding document. The problem was that few, if any, of the Soviet leaders lived in accordance with the sort of republican principles and values that would have permitted the promise of the written document to come alive in a way that could have truly served the interests and needs of the people rather than the desires of the Communist Party and its self-serving leaders.

Imam Rauf states that the United States Constitution:

"Amplified and worked out the system of government that expressed the values of the Declaration of Independence." (p. 81).

Actually, I feel there are several important senses in which Imam Rauf's claims concerning the relation of the Constitution to the Declaration of Independence are incorrect.

To begin with, the aspects of the Constitution that are most like the Declaration of Independence are: the Preamble to the Constitution, the guarantee of republican government given in Article IV, Section 4 of the Constitution, and the Bill of Rights. Without the foregoing three components, the Constitution becomes just another set of rules for divvying up power among people who want to control and direct what other people do.

Secondly, the Constitution removed one of the most important and revolutionary dimensions of the Declaration of Independence –

"The right of people to alter or abolish it" (that is, the form of government), "and to institute new Government, laying its foundation on such principles and organizing its powers in such form, as to them shall seem most likely to effect their Safety and Happiness."

Instead, the Constitution altered and diluted the nature of the aforementioned right and reduced it to being a function of elections that do nothing, for the most part, except move the dirt around during the process of transition in government.

When the Declaration of Independence mentioned the right of people to alter or abolish government, the primary focus was not on the idea of holding elections. In fact, the right to alter and abolish government is more fundamental than elections since such a right encompasses the ability to change the very nature of the principles and powers on which any given government is based. The right to alter and abolish governments concerns the character of the framework of governance itself, and that right transcends the process of merely changing the identity of the people who are elected to this or that office.

If the Constitution had been true to the spirit of the Declaration of Independence, the former would have specifically enshrined the right of the people – rather than the right of both Houses of the Congress -- to hold conventions in a manner that did not require getting the approval of the Congress and a substantial number of state governments in order to change the basic nature of government. The provisions of Article V (that is, the rules through which conventions are to be called for considering amendments to the Constitution and through which such proposed amendments are passed into law by the states) are a basic violation of the guarantee of republican government since the latter guarantee requires that those who govern should not be judges in their own cause, and, yet, any amendment that sought to change the form of government would require the members of the House to pass judgment on issues in which their own interests were at stake.

On the other hand, Article V of the Constitution concerns only the process of amending the Constitution. It says nothing about the issue of holding Constitutional Conventions for the express purpose of abolishing – rather than altering or amending -- the character of the Constitution if that Constitution is not serving the needs and interests of the people with respect to their "Safety and Happiness" – principles that are enshrined in the Preamble to the Constitution.

Thus, constitutional conventions are among the possibilities that are entailed by the Ninth and Tenth Amendments since the idea of constitutional conventions is neither one of the powers assigned to Congress, nor is it a power or right that the Constitution prohibits either to the states or to the people. Moreover, the right of the people to hold constitutional conventions (as opposed to amendment conventions) is implicit in the guarantee of republican government for the people of the respective states of the union – that is, the commitment of government to be judicious, impartial, egalitarian, unbiased, and without private passion or interests concerning the public good and welfare ... even when that public good and welfare require the dissolution or abolishment of a given form of government.

The Declaration of Independence is about people and their rights – not about the rights of states or the rights and powers of government. The Declaration of Independence is about the inalienable rights of people – not the inalienable rights of states and governments – with respect to equality, life, liberty, and the pursuit of happiness.

If not for the Bill of Rights, the unamended Constitution really doesn't have much to say about the rights and powers of people except through allusion – i.e., that which is not said and specified in the main body of the Constitution. The two exceptions to this general principle of operational character to which the unamended Constitution gives expression reside in: (1) the words of the Preamble to the Constitution that clearly indicates that the purpose of government is to serve the needs and interests of the people, and (2) the principle of the guarantee of republican government that places limits on how the people in government must conduct themselves, and, among other things, this principle requires that people in government cannot abuse, usurp, constrain, or abolish the rights and powers of people.

With the exception of the Preamble and Article IV, Section 4, the unamended Constitution really doesn't do much to address the perspective that is voiced in the Declaration of Independence. In fact, the vast majority of the unamended Constitution is not about the rights and powers of people but is, rather, largely about the rights and powers of the federal government, together with a few scraps thrown to state governments.

The Declaration of Independence is a revolutionary document. By and large, however, with the exception of Article IV, Section 4 that guarantees a republican government, and this is truly revolutionary – the unamended Constitution is not a revolutionary document, but, instead, it is a document that seeks to preserve and stabilize certain corridors of power and reserve them for government rather than for people. The amended Constitution is a revolutionary document because of the presence of the amendments of the Bill of Rights and not as a result of the Constitution, per se.

The Declaration of Independence makes claims directly for the people. At best, the unamended Constitution makes only very indirect claims for the rights of people, and even this is lost within the shuffle of elected, representative governments that frequently are not inclined to represent the people, but, rather, represent this or that: ideology, agenda, lobbyist, or power-broker. Moreover, if the obligations of central government ensuing from the guarantee of republican government – in other words, Article IV, Section 4 of the Constitution -- are not observed by the members of government, then the people end up with no rights at all even under the amended Constitution.

Democracy exists to the extent that the members of the three branches of government comply completely and vigorously with the requirements of Article IV, Section 4 of the

Constitution. The rest is just words ... words that are devoid of practical value without active, unfailing compliance with Article IV, Section 4 on the part of the members of the federal government.

On page 82 of *What's Right With Islam*, Imam Rauf writes:

"Grounding itself in reason, just as the Qur'an and the Abrahamic ethic did in asserting the self-evident oneness of God, the Declaration opens with the most important line in the document: 'We hold these truths to be self-evident.'"

There are a number of problematic issues entailed by the foregoing statement.

First, the Declaration of Independence does not open with the statement "We hold these truths to be self-evident". Instead the document opens with an account of why it is appropriate to provide an explanation for dissolving the bonds tying together two peoples ... to provide such an explanation should be done out of respect for the opinions of other human beings.

In short, the Declaration of Independence opens with an expression of republican values that give expression to qualities such as: modesty, virtue, honor, and reasonableness in relation to the opinions of others. This is done, initially, by acknowledging the right of others to be properly informed concerning the reasons for separation and dissolution of certain bonds, and, then, by providing an explanation of the list of grievances for why independence is being declared.

Working on the assumption that such documents often tend to first express those sentiments that are of highest priority to the individuals who will be signing their names to a given set of statements, the expression of republican values contained in the opening paragraph of the Declaration underlies the spirit through that the Declaration of Independence was conceived, written, signed, and delivered. It is the same spirit that is enshrined in Article IV, Section 4 of the Constitution, guaranteeing republican government to the respective states and their people.

The truths that are self-evident in the Declaration are self-evident to those who are rooted in republican values. The Declaration is addressed to all people who operate in accordance with republican values and principles.

In other words, anyone whose life is infused with qualities of: honor, integrity, character, reasonableness, judiciousness, egalitarianism, tolerance, virtue, benevolence, honesty, and impartiality will understand the nature of the self-evident truths being stated in the Declaration of Independence. However, anyone whose life was not infused with such republican values and principles would not understand the self-evident character of the truths in question.

To understand something as self-evident requires a certain receptivity and sensitivity to the principles at issue. Contrary to what Imam Rauf claims in the previous quotation, the Qur'an and the Abrahamic ethic are not primarily appeals to reason, since it is quite possible for someone to use a form of logic and reason that is unwilling to acknowledge the self-evident character of whatever principles and values are being discussed in either the Qur'an or the Abrahamic ethic.

Indeed, as Imam Rauf points out elsewhere in his book, the Prophet Abraham (peace be upon him) used reason to pursue, and become committed to, a lot of different possibilities with respect to trying to establish what might be 'self-evidently' worthy of worship. At different times in the life of Prophet Abraham (peace be upon him), different things appeared to be self-evident.

The self-evident nature of the oneness of God did not enter into the consciousness of Prophet Abraham (peace be upon him) until God had entered into his heart and made him receptive to the self-evident character of monotheism. Similarly, the self-evident nature of the principles being given expression through the Qur'an do not enter into someone's consciousness until the heart of that individual has been made receptive to such principles.

One cannot reason one's way to the self-evidence of a 'truth'. One is either open to it, or one is not.

If the character of one's understanding is oriented in the proper manner, one has insight into how human beings have a right to life, liberty, and the pursuit of happiness. If, however, one is a monarch (or someone who wishes to remain in the good graces of such a monarch) and believes in the Divine Right of Kings to control other human beings, then one might have trouble seeing the self-evident character of the sort of truths about which the Declaration of Independence speaks ... in fact, in the latter case, one is likely to see such self-evident truths as an abomination and contrary to the natural laws of the universe.

Imam Rauf states that the language of the Declaration:

"Evokes the long tradition of natural law, which holds that there is a higher law of right and wrong from which to derive human law and against which human laws might be – and ought to be – measured. It is not political will but moral reasoning accessible to all that is the foundation of the American political system." (p. 82)

If what Imam Rauf said were true, there would have been no need for the Declaration of Independence to have been written and published.

The Declaration of Independence had to be written because there was a difference of opinion concerning the nature of the 'natural' laws governing the universe. Royalty (and those loyal to royalty) believed that the authority of the king or queen to rule over other human beings was derived from a higher power – namely, God ... a higher power that had chosen royalty (and its delegates) to conduct the affairs of human beings. The signatories to the Declaration of Independence believed that the nature of the natural laws instituted by God entitled no one to govern human beings without the latter's consent and unless such governance was done in accordance with certain republican values and principles.

As Imam Rauf notes in the foregoing quote, the idea of natural law has had a long history. However, in contrast to what Imam Rauf has written in his book, the history of natural law has been entirely characterized by conflicts over, and disagreements about, the precise nature of such natural laws.

Most people – atheists and agnostics notwithstanding – agreed that whatever natural law was it was established by a higher power – namely: that which had made possible, and established, the principles through which the universe operated. Many differences arose, however, in relation to the precise nature of that natural law.

Furthermore, the moral reasoning that was to be used to translate such natural laws into principles that were (according to Imam Rauf) supposedly accessible to all tended to vary from one system of natural law to the next. Consequently, in contrast to what Imam Rauf says above, there was no unanimity of opinion concerning how to make such laws accessible to all through moral reasoning.

In a slightly different but related way, Imam Rauf makes a similar mistake earlier in his book when discussing the idea of 'din al fitrah' – a term that he translates as "natural religiousness". Imam Rauf begins with a passage from the Qur'an – namely:

"Be religious in accordance with your truest inclinations (literally, hanif-ly), the immutable nature (fitrah) of God upon which He created people – there is no altering God's creation – that is right religiousness, but most people do not know." (Surah 30, Verse 30)

The foregoing translation is somewhat problematic, because fitrah is not the immutable nature of God, but, rather, the fixed form, or 'ayn al-thabita, that constitutes the primordial potential of a human being to which the Divine idea of a given instance of fitrah gives expression. Such an ideational form is fixed and immutable, but it is not the immutable nature of God.

There is a difference between the Thinker and the thought. Although the former makes the latter possible, the thought is not Dhat, or the Divine Essence, but manifestation ... the structural or formal result that occurs when the Names and Attributes made possible by Essence shine through a given fixed form, like light through a prism -- a prism that constitutes the primordial character of the form, or Divine idea, in question.

20

Imam Rauf goes on to state:

"The idea of the verse is that any person who listens to his or her heart and conscience would recognize that God is One, that humanity is one family, that humans should be free and treat each other fairly and with justice.

"Muslims therefore call their faith din al-fitrah, "natural religiousness", meaning the goodness that flows out of human nature, action that we regard as self-evidently right and ethical ... Those who practice what their hearts tell them are therefore the right religion for them at that moment.

"God calls this natural religiosity "His own religion (din Allah, Quran 3:83, 110:2), something God has bestowed to the human critical faculties and understanding." (p. 16)

Imam Rauf is incorrect when he claims: "that any person who listens to his or her heart and conscience would recognize that God is One." The heart is a complex faculty, and not all of it is necessarily capable of correctly reflecting the truth of things.

In fact, the outermost property of the spiritual faculty known as the heart is referred to as the "qalb" in Arabic. One of the primary meanings of "qalb" is 'that which turns'.

The qalb is the battlefield on which the fight for the soul's allegiance takes place. On one side of the qalb forces such as the ego and dunya (the world created by the entanglements of our collective egos and desires) are aligned and seek to entice the heart to rebel against the truth and/or to serve non-spiritual purposes. On the other side of the qalb, the forces of spirit are aligned, and they seek to orient the heart toward truth and to induce the heart to work toward realizing the purpose of life.

The outcome of the battle is not straightforward. In fact, the outcome might not become clear until an individual's final breath is taken.

Sometimes, we listen to the qalb and it tells us, with passion, to serve the ego, the world, and non-spiritual purposes. Sometimes, we listen to the qalb and it counsels us to serve spiritual purposes.

What any given person recognizes as "self-evidently true" depends on the condition of the heart at the moment that individual looks into her or his heart. What any given person recognizes as "right and ethical" depends on the condition of the heart when one listens to what it is saying.

No matter what one's capacity for critical reasoning might be and irrespective of how intelligent an individual might be, reason's character is influenced, shaped, oriented, and colored by the condition of a person's heart. While we might all be equipped at birth with the faculties necessary to realize the nature of truth concerning our relationship with the universe, there are many forces, both within and without, that seek to undermine our innate capacities for reason and understanding and render them dysfunctional.

Having said the foregoing, let's return to the issue of republican values that were being discussed earlier. Possessing republican values and principles helped make colonists receptive to the general idea of human rights as self-evident truths.

Nonetheless, even within such a framework, the possession of these sorts of values and principles was not sufficient to generate unanimity among colonists concerning the details of natural law, and this was clearly demonstrated in relation to the many arguments, disagreements, and discussions that occurred during the ten years, or so, over which various Continental and Constitutional Conventions were held. Furthermore, the final draft of the Constitution was not unanimously accepted by all the participants in the Philadelphia Convention, nor was the ratification process a matter of universal agreement among the states.

Imam Rauf argues that:

"Nature', at least in the eyes of believers in God, is just another word for 'God's creation', and thus natural law must mean 'the laws that God established and structured creation on.' These span the spectrum from the laws of the physical sciences such as mathematics, physics, biology, and chemistry to the sociological and psychological laws that govern human relationships, all of which are knowable to humans through reason."

Imam Rauf goes on to indicate that the opening paragraph of the Declaration of Independence speaks about the "station to which the Laws of Nature and of Nature's God entitle them" and, then says:

"To Muslims, the law decreed by God is called the Shari'ah, and therefore the Laws of Nature and of Nature's God are by definition Shari'ah law." (p. 82)

Unfortunately, Imam Rauf is playing fast and loose with the form of logic and reasoning through which he is trying to establish the idea of equivalency in which the "Laws of Nature and of Nature's God" are, by definition, precisely the same with respect to both Shari'ah and the Declaration of Independence. Imam Rauf's reasoning and logic are problematic because nothing substantive has been established concerning the exact character of the 'Laws of Nature and of Nature's God" with respect to either the Declaration of Independence or Shari'ah.

What is meant by the idea of "life, liberty, and the pursuit of happiness"? What is meant by the idea of a "right"? What is meant by the "consent of the governed"? Is Shari'ah even about rights, liberty, or the consent of the governed? Is the idea of law really the best way through which to describe or engage Shari'ah? What is the precise character of the sociological and psychological laws that supposedly govern human relationships, and how do we know this? What exactly is the nature of the "station to which the Laws of Nature and of Nature's God" entitles human beings, and how do we know this?

The exploratory debate concerning the nature of the answer to all of the foregoing questions continues on. Those debates have not been settled in any universally agreed upon manner.

Even in the allegedly most objective and settled dimensions of natural law – namely, physical law – there are ongoing debates concerning the nature of the quantum world (e.g., string theory), as well as in relation to topics such as: dark energy, dark matter, the inflationary universe, the Big Bang, the physical constants, and questions concerning the origins of: life, consciousness, reason, language, and creativity. We know a few laws of nature, but the extent of our ignorance concerning even physical laws is far greater than what we know ... and the difference between the known and the unknown becomes even greater when it comes to the nature of human beings and spirituality.

The Prophet Muhammad (peace be upon him) is reported to have said:

"There are 71 sects among Jews, and only one of them is correct. There are 72 sects among Christians, and only one of them is correct. There are 73 sects among Muslims, and only one of them is correct."

So, how does one identify what constitutes the "Laws of Nature and Nature's God" amidst all of these sects?

The Prophet is reported to have said:

"God has seventy thousand veils of light and darkness."

So, how does one identify what constitutes the "Laws of Nature and Nature's God" in the midst of such veils of light and darkness?

Finally, the Prophet is reported to have said:

"Truly, the Qur'an has an outward and inward meaning, and the latter has its own inward dimension, and so on, up to seven dimensions."

So, again, how does one identify and come to know what constitutes the "Laws of Nature and

Nature's God" with respect to these different dimensions of the Qur'an?

Imam Rauf is quite wrong when he says all of the foregoing is accessible to human reason. If this were so, there would have been no need for: Revelation, the Prophetic tradition, or a process of spiritual struggle and purification. If what Imam Rauf claims were true, there would have been no sense in providing human beings with a variety of different modes of understanding and engaging reality such as the: heart (which consists of a variety of different capacities such as the qalb, breast, and fu'ad), sirr (mystery), kafi, or ruh (spirit). If Imam Rauf were correct in his foregoing assertions – which I do not believe he is – then a rational mind would have been all human beings required to realize the full nature of truth, but, as previously noted, human beings have been endowed by their Creator with far more than the faculty of reason through which to engage and understand the nature of reality and truth.

The Prophet Muhammad (peace be upon him) is reported to have said that:

"Struggle is the ordinance of God, and whatever God has ordained can only be attained through struggle."

Therefore, one needs to go through a process of struggle to properly calibrate our internal spiritual faculties so that they are able, God willing, to function properly.

Even in the realm of rational thought, not all roads lead to the truth. Furthermore, even when the exercise of such reason does lead to truth, reason has its limits with respect to its capacity to apprehend different dimensions of reality. It is only the arrogance of reason that supposes otherwise.

The foregoing perspective reflects the understanding that Sufis have espoused in various ways for hundreds of years. However, although Imam Rauf 's book, *What's Right With Islam*, often refers to the Sufi path and teachings in laudatory terms, there are many occasions in that very same book (and each of the chapters of the present collection of essays that are critical of some of Imam Rauf's ideas provide evidence for my claim in this regard) that suggest Imam Rauf sometimes doesn't seem to have much insight into the actual nature of the Sufi way, for, if he did, then I do not believe he would say many of the things that he does in his book.

For example, on pages 82-83 of his book, Imam Rauf approvingly quotes Alexander Hamilton as stating that:

"The sacred rights of mankind are not to be rummaged for among old parchments and musty records. They are written as with a sunbeam, in the whole volume of human nature, by the hand of

Divinity itself, and can never be erased or obscured by mortal power."

Imam Rauf then asks – seemingly in a rhetorical fashion – whether "the Abrahamic ethic as natural religion – Muslims' din al-fitrah as the core definition of Islam" could "be any more lucidly and evidently expressed?" [as phrased, for example, by Alexander Hamilton]

Apparently, Hamilton, when he stated the foregoing words, was ignoring or forgetting the fact that he, along with many of his fellow Framers of the Constitution, were not so successful in finding the same sacred rights for: women, Native Americans and other people of color, as well as those who were without property, inscribed into the volume of human nature ... "as if by a sunbeam". Furthermore, Imam Rauf seems to forget or ignore the fact that there are all too many Muslims who fail to find the same sacred rights inscribed in the volume of human nature in relation to: women, certain sects of other Muslims, non-Muslims, and the innocent victims of their suicide bombings.

So, to answer Imam Rauf's somewhat rhetorical question: Yes, I do believe the idea of the Abrahamic ethic as natural religion could be more lucidly and evidently stated than in the words of Alexander Hamilton.

Consider the following: What does it mean to say that Shari'ah is the law of God (and, remember, Imam Rauf often speaks in terms of "the principles that Islamic law requires of a government" (e.g., p. 80)? Most Muslims construe this to mean that Shari'ah is a legal system that regulates how people are to act and provides an array of penalties and punishments for violation of such regulations, and on many occasions, Imam Rauf seems to be in agreement with this sort of understanding.

Such a perspective cannot be true because the Qur'an clearly indicates there can be no compulsion in matters of Deen (Surah 2, Verse 256) -- that is, the process through which fitrah, or one's primordial spiritual potential, is realized. Moreover, this prohibition concerning compulsion extends to the nature of Shari'ah since this term refers to the way or path or methodology through which Deen or spirituality is realized.

The term 'shari'ah' is found only once in the Qur'an:

"O Prophet, We have put you on the Right Way (Shari'ah) concerning Deen (spirituality), so follow it, and do not yield to the desires of ignorant people." (Surah 45, Verse 18)

In Arabic, shari'ah is a noun. One of its root meanings gives reference to a place where animals come to drink water.

There is a related verb, 'shar'a' that refers to the process of taking a drink. There is a further related word, 'shaari' that could be a reference to, on the one hand, a way/path, or, on the other hand, this term could refer to someone who determines the law.

Water, the nature of water, the path to water, the drinking of water, and the purpose that the drinking of water serves all conform to the principles established by God concerning the structural character and nature of the universe. In this sense, the term shari'ah alludes to the presence of the One Who determines the nature of everything and brings together water, its nature, the path to water, the drinker, and the effects of water on the drinker to serve certain Divine purposes, and, therefore, one can speak of shari'ah as a methodology (i.e., Right Way) through which the truth of Deen or spirituality might be acquired, imbibed, and realized.

Shari'ah is not a set of legal prescriptions – although many Muslims over the years have interpreted the nature of the 'right way' through the prism of legal lenses. Shari'ah is the active place through which, if God wishes, one discovers truths concerning the nature of: reality, identity, purpose, the nature of the universe, as well as principles of justice and character.

Truth is the water to which shari'ah leads a seeker and through which one is provided with an opportunity, via a given state or station, to drink.

Shari'ah is a methodology, way, or path that gives expression to the entire set of principles, values, knowledge, and wisdom that are inherent in the Qur'an.

To try to limit the nature of shari'ah to a small set of verses of the Qur'an (i.e., various legal prescriptions that constitute less than one-tenth of Revelation) and, then, seek to force that arbitrary hermeneutic onto the collective – whether Muslim or non-Muslim – does a grave injustice to both the process of shari'ah, as well as to the complex richness, breadth, depth, and subtlety of the Qur'an. While shari'ah does involve a dimension of purification, the Qur'an provides a wealth of modalities for purifying the body, mind, heart, and soul that not only extend far beyond any set of specific legal precepts but also contain principles and values through which the public space of society might be regulated in ways that better suit the needs and problems of changing times and conditions. ... ways that people can come to agree upon through free choices rather than through being compelled to do things in a manner that is rooted in some skewed, theological, legalistic, government-serving interpretation of the Qur'an .

Whatever specific proscriptions might be given expression in the Qur'an, those proscriptions must be weighed against many other kinds of considerations, ideas, values, principles, purposes, and methods that are also given simultaneous expression in the Qur'an. How one brings the

Qur'an to bear on any given set of existential circumstances is an individual decision that is freely chosen and for which one will be held personally responsible by God. Deciding how to bring the Qur'an to bear on the challenges of life is not a collective decision whose majority view can be forcibly imposed on individuals.

The problem or challenge of how to proceed along the path of shari'ah is a matter of individual capacity, insight, discrimination, knowledge, understanding, and spiritual condition. Shura is a process of consultation with others that is recommended by the Qur'an as a way of mutually exploring important problems and issues of life, but unless a consensus is reached (which is a unanimous agreement and not merely a majority viewpoint), there is nothing except the truth that should induce a person to feel bound by the ideas and understandings of other individuals with whom one consults.

The foregoing page and a half goes to the heart of what is entailed by the Abrahamic ethic or the din al-fitrah -- the natural religion of God. It is neither a form of governance nor a set of legal proscriptions, but, rather, din al-fitrah is a methodological process for seeking the truth concerning one's essential identity and spiritual potential.

More specifically, the purpose of shari'ah or Deen is epistemic in nature. Shari'ah is not a legal system or a matter of governance.

Shari'ah is a way to knowledge concerning the nature of Deen, or spirituality. Shari'ah is a methodology through which to seek an understanding of the nature of fitrah or one's primordial potential and the relationship of such fitrah to reality and Being.

The condition of submission that, God willing, arises through the process of shari'ah is not about obedience, per se. Rather, such submission is about being prepared to accept the nature of truth that is acquired, God willing, through the process of pursuing shari'ah. In other words, the purpose of shari'ah is to provide a way through which to seek the truth, as well as a means through which to assist an individual to, God willing, modify his or her behavior, where necessary, to reflect the character of such truth.

Submission is not about bowing down to a legal system or a form of governance. Submission is a process through which one comes to acknowledge and acquiesce to the truths of existence.

An obedient servant of God is someone who lives in accordance with the requirements of truth. Just as any sincere scientist seeks to ensure that, where possible, his or her life reflects, and is in compliance with, the requirements of physical truths concerning the nature of reality, so, too, a Muslim is someone who, according to her or his spiritual capacity and condition, seeks to live life in accordance with the requirements of spiritual truths.

Quranic guidance is epistemic in nature and does not give expression to a legal system or a form of governance. That is, revelation is sent through a Messenger, or Rasul, to enlighten people and assist them to come to know about various dimensions of existence. This is why the Qur'an states that "Allah wishes to explain" (Surah 4, Verse 26 ... and there are many other Quranic verses that exemplify this point) existence to human beings and provide them with guidance in relation to the nature of: the physical world, human beings, history, identity, the nature of the Afterlife, character, faith, purpose, purification, methodology, truth, character, the Prophetic tradition, angels, jinn, faith, spiritual possibilities, society, nafs, and dunya.

God did not say that the purpose of Creation was to establish a legal system or to establish government. Rather, and as previously noted in this essay, God indicated that the purpose of Creation was rooted in God's love for Creation to come to know the nature of the Hidden Treasure.

The purpose of the basic pillars of Islam (i.e., affirming that God is the only God and Muhammad – peace be upon him – is a Prophet of God, as well as observing the requirements of prayers, fasting, charity, and pilgrimage) gives expression to modalities of purifying the inner spiritual faculties of an individual and, thereby, help ready those faculties – at least in some minimal fashion -- to be in a condition to receive whatever God wishes to disclose in the way of understanding, knowledge, insight, and unveiling. The pillars of Islam are an individual pursuit even when they are performed in conjunction with other individuals, and, as such, the purpose of those pillars is not about establishing a compulsory legal system or some form of governance.

Faith is an epistemic state – not a legal or governmental relationship – that involves a ratio between what is known and what is unknown -- a ratio that orients one to what is unknown through the character of what is known. As knowledge grows, the complex nature of the ratio between what is known and unknown also changes and, in the process, one's understanding concerning the character of existence and the nature of the universe becomes, God willing, deeper, more nuanced, and richer.

The Sufi path is a way of purification that leads, God willing, to increasingly deeper forms of understanding concerning the nature of fitrah, or one's primordial, essential spiritual potential. In other words, the Sufi path, or tasawwuf, is epistemic in nature. It is a path that pursues knowledge, understanding, wisdom, and insight concerning the nature of the human condition as well as the relation of that condition to the whole of existence. The Sufi path has nothing to do with either legal systems or forms of governance.

Consequently, irrespective of whether one is talking about: shari'ah, Deen, Islam, submission, the pillars of Islam, the Qur'an, faith, fitrah, or the Sufi path, the bottom line is always the same. All of the foregoing is rooted in pursuing and acquiring knowledge/understanding concerning the nature of the universe, and they are not rooted in legal systems or forms of governance.

Legal systems and forms of governance are human inventions that have been problematically grafted onto Islam ... oftentimes, if not usually, for the self-serving purposes of those who control, and benefit from, the existence of such legal systems and forms of government. The purpose of life is not served by learning how to comply with some given legal system or form of government. In fact, all such legal systems and forms of government tend to do is carry human beings further away from the purpose of life.

To reiterate, and to do so in the context of Imam Rauf's claims concerning what so-called Islamic law allegedly requires of government, the fact of the matter is that Islam doesn't require anything of government leaders except that they not get in the way of the right of everyone to pursue the truth concerning existence. Or, stated in another way, what Islam requires of government authorities is that they apply Islam to themselves and not assume that their task is to ensure that everyone else must understand and pursue Islam as they do.

Just as the U.S. Constitution imposes the requirements of republican values and principles upon any person who is part of the federal government, so, too, Islam imposes the obligation upon anyone who seeks to be part of government – as well as on any other Muslim -- to conduct themselves in accordance with the principles and values of Islam as an individual and not as a collective pursuit. In fact, if one lists the qualities of republicanism, these are remarkably similar to the character traits that any good Muslim should have and exhibit in her or his relationships with other people – namely, honesty, honor, integrity, benevolence, modesty, independence, egalitarianism, judiciousness, virtuousness, tolerance, reasonableness, impartiality, and being high-minded (and, therefore, is not done out of self-serving motivations) in conjunction with advancing the public good and welfare.

Republican principles and values are not about legalisms or governance. They are a way of life ... a way of behaving in relation to other people.

Similarly, Islam is not about legalisms or governance. Islam is a way of life that entails, among other things, a way of behaving in relation to other people.

On page 104 of *What's Right With Islam*, Imam Feisal states:

"Having come to America for religious liberty, the founders were concerned that the powers of state might be used to further one religion above any other, to enforce one religious set, doctrine, or interpretation over another, or to harm religious establishment. The separation of church and state was intended to mean that the state might not prejudicially side for, or against, any one religion or church."

To claim that people – especially the Framers of the Constitution -- came to America to find religious liberty is, at best, misleading and very incomplete. To be sure, there were some whose primary motivation for journeying to America might have been to escape from religious persecution, but the primary motivations were more likely to be political, economic, and personal, rather than for religious reasons.

The New World was synonymous with opportunity … opportunities for gaining wealth, property, economic power, and starting over. The New World was an opportunity to get out from under the classed oppression that dominated Europe. The New World was about pursuing dreams and seeking to fulfill individual potential in ways that, for the most part, were not even imaginable in Europe.

The First Amendment was not primarily about religious freedom, but, rather, it was about political freedom. It was directed toward ensuring that the central government could not control important freedoms concerning belief, speech, the press, assembly, and the ability to petition government in relation to grievances against the government.

The First Amendment – along with the other nine amendments of the Bill of Rights --was intended to ensure that the promise of the New World could not be taken away by central government. Religious freedom was only one concern among many other political anxieties that were intended to help Americans avoid the many problems of governance that plagued Europe and other parts of the world.

In fact, the manner in which the initial part of the First Amendment is worded suggests something that might, or might not, have escaped the imaginations of the Framers of the Constitution along with imaginations of many Constitutional analysts and commentators since the inception of the that amendment. More specifically, the initial part of the First Amendment states: "Congress shall make no law respecting an establishment of religion, or prohibiting the free exercise thereof."

All of the Framers of the Constitution had some form of religious orientation, ranging from the theologically minimalist character of Deism to the liberalism and tolerance of Universalist teachings, or to the singular Roman Catholicism of Daniel Carroll of Maryland, or to the peaceful, gentle tenacity of Quaker discipline, as well as to a variety of other Protestant traditions. In view of the foregoing, one needs to ask a very important question: If religion – of whatever description – was an orienting and influential force in the lives of such individuals, then wouldn't it follow that when such people became involved in central government – and not all Framers of the Constitution went on to be part of the federal government – then whatever public policy issued from them was, in a very real sense, a form of establishing religion because such public policy was a reflection of their understanding concerning the nature of the relationship of human beings to Divinity?

Moreover, one can expand the character of this question. Assuming that people of all different varieties of belief – overtly religious or not – seek to act in accordance with what they hold to be most fundamental and true concerning the nature of reality and that all people seek to pursue to fulfill the potential of being human as they understand such potential, isn't there a sense in which all public policy is rooted in a theory about truth and reality that shares many characteristics with religion?

If "life, liberty, and the pursuit of happiness" are inalienable rights that have been inscribed in the hearts of all human beings by their Creator, then the manner in which one exercises choice in relation to "life, liberty, and the pursuit of happiness" is also rooted in religious values and principles. While the First Amendment clearly indicates that Congress can make no law prohibiting the free exercise of religion, a problem arises in conjunction with the provision of the First Amendment that stipulates that "Congress might make no law respecting an establishment of religion" since pretty much everything that the members of Congress do is framed by, and oriented through, the filters of their personal beliefs concerning the nature of human potential and the universe in relation to the Creator, and, therefore, constitutes an "establishment of religion".

Agnostics and atheists fare no better under the First Amendment. Even when one does not believe in God or one is uncertain about whether, or not, God exists, the beliefs an agnostic or atheist holds have a sacred quality to them in much the same way as religious beliefs do. Those beliefs are fundamental and sacrosanct and are considered – rightly or wrongly – to be the key to the pursuit of "life, liberty, and the pursuit of happiness" and have been endowed to them by their Creator – that is nature or evolution.

If Buddhism – which does not contain the idea of a personal Deity (although there is a distinction that sometimes is drawn between 'self-power' and 'other-power') – can be considered a religion, then atheism and agnosticism also constitute systems of belief concerning the nature of the essential, fundamental nature of life's mysterious, sacred qualities and, as such, are religious in character. Or, approached in another way, atheism and agnosticism are responses to certain kinds of religious beliefs, and, therefore, define themselves in terms of a form of religiousness that rejects the idea of a personal God Who has created the universe and to Whom human beings have any responsibility or obligation.

Like other forms of religion, atheism and agnosticism give expression to a system of beliefs that describe and attempt to explain a philosophy of life that concerns the nature of the universe and the place of human beings in that universe. Trying to refer to atheism or agnosticism as philosophies rather than religions cannot hide the many parallels between religion and philosophy and, as a result, indicates that labeling atheism and agnosticism as expressions of philosophy rather than as expressions of religion is rather an extremely arbitrary exercise.

In fact, atheists and agnostics are likely to view religion as nothing more than bad philosophy. Therefore, they see religion as an exercise that addresses all of the same problems, questions, and issues concerning existence that atheists and agnostics do, but religion, they believe, does so in problematic ways.

Consequently, atheism and agnosticism are engaged in very similar sorts of epistemological and moral engagement of existence as people of religion are so engaged. As a result, the First Amendment applies to atheists and agnostics as much as it does to any other kind of activity that, broadly speaking, falls within the sphere of concerns and interests as religion does.

The public policy agendas of atheists and agnostics are every bit as much rooted in their fundamental beliefs concerning the nature of existence, as are the public policy agendas of other forms of religion. Such systems of fundamental belief concerning the nature of human beings, life, existence, and the universe are precisely the kind of system of thought that the First Amendment sought to exclude from being established into law via Congress.

Individuals – not government – have the right to pursue such ideas concerning the nature of "life, liberty, and the pursuit of happiness". Moreover, the exercise of the foregoing right is circumscribed by the condition that an equivalent right is being extended to all other individuals. Therefore, the exercise of one's basic philosophy or religion cannot be pursued in such a way that would prohibit or prevent other people from being able to seek "life, liberty, and the pursuit of happiness" in their own way.

Some might object to the foregoing analysis by saying that if government were to operate in the manner indicated – that is, without being able to propose and institute agendas of public policy -- then it could not pass any legislation whatsoever because everything would be an expression of a public policy that was rooted in an activity – namely, religion broadly conceived – which was constrained by the First Amendment. Under such circumstances, one might wish to ask: What would be the point of government?

One could answer the foregoing question by saying: "exactly". However, I do believe there is a point to government, and it is a process of seeking to inclusively engage all of society through assisting everyone to find relatively harmonious ways of seeking "life, liberty, and the pursuit of happiness", as well as instituting ways of protecting their right to do so.

There are conflicting tendencies at the heart of the U.S. Constitution. On the one hand, the <u>unamended</u> Constitution is largely about the ways of power – who gets it; what it can be used for; how one can lose it; as well as how power is to be divided up among: the three branches of federal government, along with the respective power centers in the various states. On the other hand, the <u>amended</u> Constitution is about the rights of people in relation to such power.

The bridge between the two comes in the form of the Preamble – which stipulates what the federal government is supposed to be doing with its power to assist the people in their activities concerning "life, liberty, and the pursuit of happiness" and in Article IV, Section 4 concerning how power is to be exercised – namely, in compliance with, and conformity to, republican values and principles.

Unfortunately, American democracy has largely descended into a frenzied and insane struggle to – like the Golum of Tolkien's *Lord of the Rings* Trilogy -- win the 'ring of power' through whatever means are deemed necessary and, in the process, forget about, if not trample upon, the Preamble, the requirement of guaranteeing republican government, and the Bill of Rights. American democracy, in other words, has become a chaotic, discordant, and uncivil manifestation of all the worst, least endearing qualities human beings have to offer.

Imam Rauf claims that:

"Pluralism of religion and churches is the foundation of the establishment clause. This is similar to the Islamic injunction in the Qur'an: " Say: O disbelievers: To you your religion, and to me mine." (Surah 109, Verse 6).

I disagree with Imam Rauf's foregoing interpretation in a number of respects.

In line with the foregoing discussion, the heart of the establishment clause is a constraint on government. Government shall neither establish nor prohibit the exercise of religion.

The point of the initial part of the First Amendment is not to promote or encourage pluralism of religion. Rather, the purpose of the amendment is to ensure that government does not seek to impose religious beliefs of any kind on the citizenry. The First Amendment is not about what citizens can do with respect to religion, but, rather, it is about what government cannot do in relation to religion.

The whole purpose of the Declaration of Independence and the Bill of Rights is to assert that no government or system of laws has the right to impose itself on human beings, because human beings, unlike governments and systems of laws, possess certain inalienable rights. Governments should exist only with the consent of those who freely choose to place certain kinds of constraints upon their inalienable rights via the agency of government.

Furthermore, the Quranic Verse or ayat that Imam Rauf cites in the context of his discussion of religious pluralism does not say what he claims it says. He uses the verse – "Say: O disbelievers: To you your religion, and to me mine." (Surah 109, Verse 6) – as an expression of religious pluralism, but, in reality, the Quranic verse is merely saying that people choose their own form of religion and that the religion of those individuals who are not committed to the truth is not the same as the religion of those who submit to the truth.

Imam Rauf goes on to say:

"Pluralism within religion developed in the field of Islamic law as Muslim scholars recognized that differing interpretations on a number of issues could be maintained while still adhering to the letter and spirit of the Quranic and Prophetic legal injunctions and their core prescriptions. All the Muslim schools of law (madhhabs) recognized each other as equally valid." (p. 104).

Aside from my previous comments concerning the perspective that neither Islam nor the Qur'an constitutes a legal system or form of governance, I would add a further observation concerning the above quote from Imam Rauf. Although all Muslim schools of law might recognize one another as equally valid, one wonders what the criteria of validity are for forming schools of law that are to be imposed on human beings, whether Muslim or non-Muslim.

What Muslim theologians and legalists have done in creating schools of laws is the antithesis of the principles being set forth in the Declaration of Independence and the Bill of Rights. Such theologians and legalists have sought -- and actually have done so in opposition to the purposes for which such schools of thought were originally established – to set up systems of laws and governance that are to be imposed on people without the consent of the latter and in direct violation of God's directive that there is to be no compulsion in matters of Deen or spirituality.

While Imam Rauf might be correct in asserting that the various schools of Muslim law recognize the validity of one another's approach to legal interpretations of the Qur'an and Islam, one can question whether, or not, any of those schools are valid in the eyes of God. In fact, any Muslim might legitimately say to those theologians and legalists – "To you your religion, and to me mine" – and demand to be left alone by such systems of law.

The various schools of law recognize the validity of one another's approach to the issue of law because they all have made the same mistake and have entered into a sort of conspiracy – or, perhaps, 'complicity' would be a better term -- with one another to try to convince the generality of Muslims that the latter must obey one, or another, of the schools of law, when the Qur'an clearly indicates that one must only obey, and be in compliance with, the truth, and such obedience can never be compelled but must be freely chosen by an individual.

People are free to choose submission to the truth, and they are free to choose submission to other than the truth. Shari'ah is the journey of exploration that seeks to discover spiritual truth and, once realized, provides an array of possibilities (methods of remembrance, purification, and worship) that are intended to assist individuals to comply with the requirements of such truth according to one's capacity to do so. Shari'ah has nothing to do with becoming obedient to a particular theory of legalistic hermeneutic or interpretation concerning the nature of Islam.

The conspiracy or condition of complicity in which the different Muslim schools of law are immersed is like that of people who privately get together, arrange power sharing among themselves, and, then, demand that the general public must submit to their system for exercising power. Such power-sharing arrangements (whether by the inventors of various systems of governance or the inventors of various systems of law) tend to be inherently opposed to the inalienable rights of people.

Imam Rauf asserts on page 105 of *What's Right with Islam* that:

"The principles of rule laid down by the Prophet and his four successors show that the Islamic conception of state is not one in which Islam in the liturgical sense has to be held as the state religion but rather that the state must be a religious state, in which God is the ultimate ruler."

Neither the Prophet nor the four individuals who assumed leadership within the Muslim community were thinking in any way remotely along the lines of the modern conception of state – Islamic or otherwise. The Prophet did not go to Medina with the idea of establishing a state.

As a person who was respected by most of the people in Medina he became the de facto head of a tribal society in an urban environment. When people came to him and insisted that he decide some matter, or other, he complied with the wish and did so as a Prophet and not as a head of state while simultaneously encouraging the people to address their concerns, problems, and sins to God.

When the Prophet negotiated an agreement – sometimes referred to as a Constitution – among the different tribes in and around Medina, this negotiation was undertaken for purposes of establishing some ground rules among tribally diverse peoples with varying beliefs in order to establish a set of common and reciprocal understandings concerning their interaction with one another. It was not the constitution for a new state.

Upon conquering Mecca, the Prophet did not proclaim himself as the new ruler of a state that consisted of Mecca and Medina. Rather, he appointed local people – some of whom were former enemies -- to become leaders of the community and left for Medina.

After the armed conflict with the Quraish tribe and their allies had ended, the Prophet sent out emissaries to invite people to Islam. He did this in conjunction with his responsibilities as God's Rasul (Messenger) and Nabi (Prophet) and not as the head of a state.

When the Prophet ordered his army to wage war against those who slew or mistreated his emissaries, he did not do this as the head of a state. He did this as the head of an ummah or community of believers who had the right to be protected from such attacks.

The Prophet was never the head of an Islamic state. He was a Muslim whose character and spiritual mission commanded respect and whose spiritual qualities influenced the surrounding community to behave in some ways rather than others.

The ties that bound the Prophet to the community, and vice versa, were not those of a legal system or a system of governance. The ties were of a spiritual nature and manifested themselves in qualities of tolerance, forgiveness, patience, charitableness, friendship, honesty, nobility, judiciousness, integrity, love, benevolence, reasonableness, reciprocity, egalitarianism, and self-sacrifice.

The foregoing qualities are somewhat similar to the values and principles that are inherent in the republican values and principles that were so prized by the Framers of the Constitution. When successive federal governments in the United States marginalized the Constitutional guarantee of republican government, democracy began to run aground in America. When the Muslim community began to abandon the Islamic qualities of character and spirituality that tied Muslims together, the community began to run aground throughout the Muslim world.

It took less than 60 years for democracy to go missing in the United States following the ratification of the Constitution. It took less than 60 years for Islam to go missing in the Muslim world following the passing away of the Prophet.

In the case of democracy, republican values and principles that were rooted in a belief in spiritual understandings became lost in a scramble for power. In the case of Islam, the principles of moral character (the Prophetic model) that were rooted in a spiritual understanding had also become lost in a scramble for power.

Neither republican principles nor Islamic principles of character were ever about governance, legal systems, or the state. They were codes of personal conduct through which one interacted with other people and treated them in accordance with the inalienable rights that are inherent in human nature.

There is no concept of an Islamic state in the Qur'an. What is present in the Qur'an is guidance concerning how to treat other human beings – whether believers or non-believers.

When people who became leaders of a Muslim community operated in accordance with the Prophetic model of conduct, such a community tended to become stable and flourish. When people who became leaders in America operated in accordance with the values and principles of republican philosophy, democracy tended to become stable and flourish.

The common factor in all of this is not the existence of a state, or a constitution, or a Bill of

Rights, or a given school of Muslim law. The deciding factor is the quality of character through which people -- both leaders and citizens -- conduct their lives in relation to one another.

States cannot force people to have character. Constitutions cannot force people to have character. Muslim schools of law cannot force people to have character.

Only when shari'ah – in a democratic sense or in an Islamic sense -- is pursed in a sincere, persistent, rigorous, and unbiased fashion is character likely to arise. Successful states and legal systems presuppose the existence of such character. They do not generate it.

Thus, when Imam Rauf states (and previously quoted) that:

"The Islamic conception of state is not one in which Islam in the liturgical sense has to be held as the state religion but rather that the state must be a religious state, in which God is the ultimate ruler ..."

I believe he is incorrect.

He is incorrect because, and as already had been noted, there really is no Islamic conception of a state. Moreover, Imam Rauf is incorrect because, on the one hand, there is no need for a state if God is truly the ruler of the hearts within a community, and, if God is not the ruler of the hearts in such a community, then, no state – Islamic or otherwise –

will be able to change the condition of such a people.

There is a further problem with the foregoing quote from Imam Rauf's book. More specifically, what does it mean to say that a state is religious and that God is the ultimate ruler of such a state?

There are many, many approaches to, and theories about, what is entailed by the idea of being religious. When the Taliban prevent women from being educated, they think they are being religious. When police in Saudi Arabia prevent young girls from escaping a fire because the young women do not conform to the police's idea of a proper dress code, the police believe they are being religious. When suicide bombers take innocent lives, the bombers are convinced they are being religious. When theologians issue a fatwa that says it is okay for Muslims to kill other Muslims, they think they are being religious ... as does the Imam who included such a fatwa in his book and recommended that *The New York Times* print the fatwa. When Muslims commit so-called honor killings, they believe they are being religious. When Muslims practice infibulations – female genital mutilation – they think they are being religious. When the leaders of the medieval Inquisition tortured and killed people, those leaders believed they were being religious. When the kings and queens of Europe operated in accordance with the idea of the 'Divine right of Kings' and, in the process, killed, imprisoned, tortured, and exploited people around the world, the members of royalty believed they were being religious. When Christian right-to-lifers deprive those who work in abortion clinics of the latter's lives and enthusiastically support their (i.e., the right-to-lifers) military's killing of thousands of innocent women, children and men in Afghanistan or Iraq, the former individuals believe they are being religious. When white slavers abused, tortured, killed, and raped Black people, the former believed they were being religious and acting in accordance with God's rule. When Jews violate international law and occupy territory belonging to another people, or build walls, or steal the property of others and build settlements on such property, or deprive people of water, or kill innocent Palestinians, or bulldoze the homes of Palestinians, they believe they are being religious. When Hindus kill Muslims, or Muslims kill Hindus, they both believe they are being religious. When Americans kill Native people, steal Native lands, prevent Native people from practicing their faith, and sexually or physically abuse young Native children in boarding schools, the former believe they are being religious. When Catholic bishops and cardinals protect priests who have sexually molested innocent children by re-locating those priests and, through tactics of stealth, move such pedophiles into other communities where the same activities occur again, the former individuals believe they are being religious.

All of the foregoing perpetrators of crimes believe that they have the right to do what they do because they believe that God is the ultimate ruler of the state, and, therefore, they have the right to do what they do because they are operating in accordance with their understanding of what it means to claim that God is the ultimate ruler of their state. People can rationalize all manner of self-serving horror in the name of God, and in this way, they believe that such behavior is entailed by what it means to be religious.

Imam Rauf cites a 2002 quote of Antonin Scalia, the Supreme Court Justice to better convey what the author of *What's Right With Islam* is getting at when the Imam talks about what it means to say that a state is religious and that God is the ultimate ruler of such a state. More specifically, in paraphrasing Justice Scalia, Imam Rauf says:

"That even if we declare government in the most limited way as "lawfully constituted authority" or "lawfully constituted authority that rules justly", such government "derives its moral authority from God." (p. 106)

What is meant by the idea of "lawfully constituted authority"? For most of the history of the United States, Congress, the Executive Office, and the Supreme Court have not been in compliance with the requirements of Article IV, Section 4 of the Constitution – a section that guarantees republican government to the respective states. For most of the history of the United States, Congress, the Executive Office, and the Supreme Court have deprived the people of their Ninth and Tenth Amendment Rights.

Even if one were to assume that a government is lawfully constituted according to the electoral requirements of a constitutional document, that government is not exercising "lawfully constituted authority" if it does not abide by the other requirements of that same constitutional document. Moreover, if such an allegedly "lawfully constituted authority" does not act in accordance with the requirements of various constitutional provisions, then, one cannot assume that such "lawfully constituted authority" is ruling in a "just" manner.

The foregoing perspective of Justice Scalia is predicated on an array of questionable assumptions. Among such questionable assumptions are ones concerning the issue of whether, or not, a government that is allegedly based on "lawfully constituted authority" actually acts in compliance with the authority through which it is constituted, as well as the issue of whether or not the rulings that are made by the government -- which supposedly is rooted in "lawfully constituted authority" --actually are just. According to what criteria of justice and according to what theory of justice, and according to what sorts of proof can one say that such governments are acting in a just manner?

Furthermore, Justice Scalia makes an unwarranted logical leap when he claims that when you have a government that is supposedly based on "lawfully constituted authority" or when you have such a government that allegedly rules in a "just" way, then, according to Justice Scalia, this means that such a government "derives its moral authority from God". Until one knows the conditions and criteria for judging whether, or not, a government actually is based on "lawfully constituted authority", and until one knows the conditions and criteria for judging whether, or not, various rulings are just, and until one knows whether, or not, such authority and rulings are actually in conformity with God's view of authority and justice, then, one is not really in a position to justify the claim that such a government derives its moral authority from God.

Imam Rauf further points out how Justice Scalia cites:

"... the apostle Paul in Romans 13:1-5 (but making a point that Muslims and people of most religions subscribe to), he [that is, Paul] says that every human soul is subject to the powers ordained by God, and that to resist them is to resist the ordinance of God." (p. 106)

Once again, this is argument by assumption – on the part of Justice Scalia, Paul, and Imam Rauf).

Without specifying what the powers are that allegedly are ordained by God, and without providing incontrovertible proof that such powers have, indeed, been ordained by God, then one is not in a position to justifiably claim that anyone who resists such an assertion is resisting the ordinance of God. Many people claim God's authority for what they are saying and, in the process, allude to the idea that whoever resists such "leaders" is resisting an ordinance of God. Yet, when pressed, such "leaders" are not able to demonstrably justify their claim as being anything other than a claim that assumes its own truth.

Imam Rauf proceeds to add a further quote from Antonin Scalia:

"The reaction of people of faith to this tendency of democracy to obscure the divine authority behind government should not be resignation to it, but the resolution to combat it as effectively as possible."

A short while later, Imam Rauf states:

"In other words, the founders intended America to be a religious society and nation, a society whose ethics emanate from our religious beliefs ... Our government's moral authority derives from the Constitution whose moral basis is God's law." (p. 106)

The words of both Justice Scalia and Imam Rauf are very dangerous. Their words are dangerous because the two individuals seek to assert – without any semblance of reliable or plausible proof -- that God is the authority for everything that a government does and because they are making assumptions about whether, or not, a given government is based upon "lawfully constituted authority" or whether, or not, the rulings issued through such a government are "just". Such a perspective helps to construct a very slippery and dangerous slope in which someone's ideas about religion, government, and justice get confused for, and conflated with, Divinity's perspective concerning human beings ... a confusion and conflation that can serve as the door through which all manner of injustice, abuse, and exploitation are heaped upon citizens and non-citizens by a government that allegedly is based upon "lawfully constituted authority".

The perspective being advanced by Justice Scalia and Imam Rauf is also incorrect in the following sense. Whatever the religious beliefs of the Framers of the Constitution might have been, the telltale indicator that they had no intention of requiring the nation or its government to be religious in nature is given expression through Article IV, Section 4 of the Constitution.

The aforementioned section of the Constitution does not require the federal government to guarantee the respective states of the Union a Christian government or a religious government or a government that seeks to act in compliance with the ordinances of God. Instead, Article IV, Section 4 of the Constitution requires the central government to guarantee republican government – that is, a government that is run in accordance with the values and principles of republicanism such as: impartiality, honor, reasonableness, honesty, self-sacrifice, benevolence, judiciousness, egalitarianism, integrity, character, virtuousness, tolerance, modesty, and independence of thought.

One does not have to believe in God to be committed to the principles of republicanism. Commitment to republican values and principles requires only that a person interact with other people in a way that reflects the republican philosophy with respect to how human beings should be treated – whether in relation to government, in particular, or social concourse, in general.

Republicanism was a child of the 18th Century Enlightenment. Republican philosophy was an exercise in the use of reason to fashion ideas about governance and social interaction.

Republican philosophy might have appealed to people of a spiritual or religious inclination because the values and principles of republicanism often tended to coincide and overlap with various spiritual and religious beliefs concerning the nature of morality and social justice. Republican philosophy might even have been framed, to some extent, by the spiritual and religious filters of various thinkers, but republican values and principles were never intended to constitute a religious system of any kind. Rather, they were intended as a prescription for establishing civility in governance and in social interactions.

Republican values and principles were a kind of etiquette or set of manners through which one engaged other people in a civilized fashion. Whether, or not, one was a religious person, one was expected to act in accordance with republican values and principles in order to be considered a civilized person and to be considered a person of reason.

In addition, to suppose that republican values and principles were primarily of a religious nature would have been to violate the spirit of the Establishment Clause of the First Amendment. In other words, if the guarantee of republican government that is given expression in Article IV, Section 4 of the Constitution is nothing more than a set of code words for religious beliefs, principles, and values, then what Article IV, Section 4 is requiring the central government to do is to violate the First Amendment, because requiring government to guarantee republican government from such a perspective would have constituted an establishment of religion by Congress.

Imam Rauf cites the Qur'an at this point in an attempt to support his position concerning the imperative to obey the requirements of government. He points out that in Surah 4, Verse 59, one finds:

"Obey God and obey the messenger and those in authority from among you."

Imam Rauf does not give the full verse in the foregoing quote. Following what he cites, the Qur'an goes on to indicate:

"... then if you quarrel about anything, refer it to Allah and the Apostle if you believe in Allah and the Last Day; this is better and very good in the end."

There is nothing in the Quranic verse that talks about taking whatever differences might arise among the people concerning this or that issue and, then, referring them to those in authority among them. Differences are to be referred to Allah and to the Apostle.

What is meant by: the process of "referring" such differences to Allah and the Apostle? Well, if one lived in the time of the Prophet, then one could have asked him directly, or one could have referred one's concerns directly to Allah ... and the Prophet often encouraged people to take their concerns to Allah directly rather than bring them to him.

With respect to people who live now, the Qur'an does not suggest that we should take our differences to the ones in authority from among us. Rather, the guidance is still to refer such matters to Allah and the Apostle. This can be done, but it is a spiritual process, not a legal one or a matter of governance.

Of course, there are entire schools of Muslim law that try to argue that the way in which one, in this day and age, refers differences of opinion concerning spirituality to the Prophet is by going through his sayings or hadiths and attempting to establish how they believe the Prophet would have ruled with respect to such differences on the basis of those sayings. This entire enterprise is presumptuous in the extreme.

Even if one were to agree that all the sayings attributed to the Prophet and that have been compiled by various individuals were veridical or true, stating a saying says nothing about what the intention of the Prophet was when he said what he is reported to have said. Was the intention specific to the people being addressed in the saying, or was the intention of a more universal nature? How would we ever be able to determine that might be the case?

Moreover, one also is being presumptuous to try and claim that if the Prophet were physically present today, he would have issued a ruling that is precisely the same as what is being issued through this or that school or law in relation to this or that set of circumstances. One is being equally presumptuous to suppose that one's interpretation of the Qur'an is so impeccable that one has the right to impose that interpretation on other people.

In order to bolster his argument that people are required to obey government, Imam Rauf states three sayings of the Prophet.

(1) "My community will not come to a consensus on a wrong, and if you disagree, follow the largest group";

(2) "It is your duty to stand by the united community and the majority";

(3) "The hand of God is upon the majority."

So, is Imam Rauf saying that if the largest group of Muslims in one's community advocate: honor killings, or suicide bombings, or infibulations (female genital mutilation), or slavery; or treating women as second and third class citizens, then, in effect, this means that the Prophet is saying that one has a duty to stand by the majority and that the hand of God is upon such a majority? Is Islam really to be pursued in accordance with polling data and irrespective of what such a majority is advocating?

Is Imam Rauf claiming that when the United States government decides to oppress and exploit: Natives, Blacks, people of color, women, and the poor, or when the United States government decides to kill innocent people – whether directly or through surrogates -- in: Iraq, Afghanistan, Lebanon, Palestine, Vietnam, Guatemala, Panama, Chile, Cambodia, El Salvador, Haiti, and Nicaragua, then, the Prophet is counseling us that we have a duty to stand by such a majority and that the hand of God is upon such a majority? Surely, this would be a perversion of everything that Islam teaches.

In addition, whatever the Prophet might have meant or intended in relation to the words that are attributed to him in the three hadiths or sayings that were cited above, what Imam Rauf does not include in his discussion another directive of the Prophet. More specifically, on a number of different occasions, the Prophet also said that people should not keep collections of his sayings, and this is on the authority of a number of people, including one of his closest companions and father-in-law, Abu Bakr Siddiq (may Allah be pleased with him).

By and large, Muslims abided by the Prophet's directive with respect to the issue of not keeping or maintaining collections of Hadith until a time more than two hundred years (beginning with Bukhari) after the passing away of the Prophet. Yet, Imam Rauf apparently feels he is justified – even though what he claims is in direct contravention to what the Prophet indicated more than 1400 years ago (that is, in relation to keeping collections of hadiths) -- and, then goes even further, by claiming that the words of the Prophet said 1400 years ago are intended as counsel to Muslims today with respect to the issue of obeying those in authority within government – no matter what evil those in authority might be doing -- and that Muslims have a duty to stand by the majority irrespective of what that majority does and that the hand of God is upon the majority irrespective of what that majority advocates.

One of the many problems that I have with *What's Right With Islam* is the essential disconnect that seems to exist between different parts of his book. For instance, at certain points in his work (e.g., pages 113-115), Imam Rauf describes how, on the one hand, Islam is a path of personal spiritual commitment through which individuals seek to come to understand the nature of things, including themselves, and how, on the other hand, any attempt to make Islam a collective system of religion is "dangerous" and is likely to lead to conflict and sectarian problems. However, at other points in the same book (e.g., page 105 -107), Imam Rauf appears to claim that Muslims have a duty to follow the authority of the majority and to obey government.

According to Imam Rauf, the idea of "religion" has undergone a transition in meaning. More specifically:

"Religion, which once referred to acting piously, became known instead as an identity. Religion changed from something you did into something that you were. Instead of owning your religion (as an act that you do) and being responsible for your actions (your acts of religiosity), you instead belonged to your religion; it became something that owns you." (p. 115)

To say – as Imam Rauf does on pages 105-107 - - that one has a duty to follow the authority of the majority and that one must obey government leaders is, in effect, to say that the majority and the government own you. Moreover, if an individual is owned by: the majority and/or the government, then one is no longer in a position to pursue Islam as an individual, spiritual commitment with respect to the seeking of truth about the nature of reality.

Under such circumstances, one's identity becomes defined by being a member of the majority and/or by being an obedient servant of government. Instead of owning one's religion, one becomes owned by the religion, and this is precisely the position against which Imam Rauf argues toward the beginning of the very next chapter of his book. Thus, in a very essential way, Imam Rauf seems to be at odds with himself in his book as he, simultaneously espouses points of view that are contradictory in relation to each other.

Throughout *What's Right With Islam*, Imam Rauf seeks to draw favorable parallels between constitutional democracy and Islam in the sense that he often tends to argue that Islam and constitutional democracy operate in similar ways and are motivated by similar purposes involving themes of liberty, individualism, concern for one's neighbors, and so on. Nonetheless, as Imam Rauf also occasionally points out in contradistinction to the foregoing theme, Islam is not really a form of governance, but instead, it is a way of individually pursuing, and, God willing, submitting to, the realization of the truth concerning one's relationship with the nature of reality.

I believe that Imam Rauf often confuses, if not conflates, spiritual issues with matters of governance. Indeed, as indicated previously, he seems, at times, to want to make spirituality a function either of what the majority maintain and/or a function of what those in authority decide in relation to how the collective should be governed.

For example, Imam Rauf starts out in Chapter 4 (Where the Devil Got in the Details) of *What's Right With Islam* talking about the idea of Islam being a "personal commitment to God". (p. 113) With certain reservations, I tend to agree with that statement.

Creation was not generated through any need that God had for human commitment. Creation was a pure act of Grace (in other words, it was totally undeserved) that provided an endlessly rich and structurally complex opportunity for the participants of Creation to explore their respective potentials or capacities in relation to the nature of Creation and to be thankful for such an opportunity.

As is said in a Hadith Qudsi (utterances that are manifested through the voice of the Prophet Muhammad – peace be upon him – but that actually are the words of Divinity being spoken through the Prophet): "I was a hidden treasure and loved to be known, so I brought forth Creation." Existence is the venue through which human beings come to know the truth about, and reality of, the Divine Treasure according to an individual's capacity to know and according to God's Mercy with respect to engendering such knowledge.

No aspect of creation – including a human being – is capable of circumscribing and exhausting Divinity. We know of God's treasure only what God chooses to disclose and, then, only in accordance with the capacity of the one to whom such disclosures are given.

Human beings were not created for the sake of being committed to God but were created for the sake of becoming immersed in the truth and reality encompassed by the infinite manifestations made possible by the underlying Hidden Treasure of Divinity. Islam is the process of submitting to the truth and reality of Being. Islam is the process of submitting to the purposes for which Creation was generated ... to come to know the nature of the Hidden Treasure that is distributed across and through every realm of Being.

The Qur'an states: "I have not created human beings nor jinn except that they might worship Me. (Surah 51, Verse 56)

The essence of worship is knowledge. To know (and not just believe) that Creation is just one miniscule, yet incredible manifestation, of the infinite Hidden Treasure and to understand the nature of one's relationship with Creation is to be in a state or station of worship. To act upon such knowledge is to give expression to worship.

In true worship there is no commitment to anything – for that would indicate separation from the truth. In true worship, there is only the realized experience of the knowledge concerning rootedness in reality that is being given expression through one's acts or behavior ... a rootedness that is infinitely nuanced and that, according to the Sufis, is never repeated in precisely the same way.

The Qur'an indicates that:

"Lo! Ritual worship preserves from lewdness and iniquity, but, verily, remembrance of Allah is more important." (Surah 29, Verse 45)

Thus, committing oneself to ritual forms of worship (i.e., the five pillars of Islam) plays an important role in helping to cleanse impurities that obscure and prevent an individual from acquiring, a deeper understanding of the nature of truth and reality. Nonetheless, 'remembering' the truth and reality of Being is more important, and remembrance is not a commitment but constitutes epistemological and experiential states and stations of manifested Being.

Divinity underlies the truth and reality of all things. Therefore, truth and reality are but manifestations that reflect the Divine Treasure that makes such manifestations possible.

We can know Divine manifestation in an essential way, but we cannot know God in any essential way. This reflects the nature and limits of Creation.

We seek God because God is the source and means through which all understanding and knowledge concerning our relationship to the Hidden Treasure is realized. We worship God because God's Hidden Treasure manifests truth and reality, and the greater one's understanding and knowledge concerning such truth and reality, then the deeper and purer is the nature of one's worship of the truth. We remember God because it is only through the process of remembrance that God brings one into contact with the nature of human potential – or fitrah – in relation to the Hidden Treasure. We should have no other god but God before us, because truth and reality only can be found through the Source of truth and reality, and all that 'other than God' can do is lead one to delusional states – As the Qur'an indicates: "... and what is there after the Truth save error?" (Surah 10, Verse 32) We give thanks to God because, if not for Divine Mercy and Generosity, there would be: no opportunity, no Hidden Treasure, no knowledge, no purpose, and no possibility for the realization of human potential

God is simultaneously independent of creation and intimately connected with it. God is independent of us because Divinity does not depend on human beings for anything.

God does not need us to seek Divinity. God does not need human worship. Goes not need us to remember Divinity.

Human beings are the ones who need to seek, worship, and remember God. For seeking, worshiping, and remembrance are the sine qua non for unlocking human potential and, thereby, realizing the purpose of Creation and the purpose of one one's existence within that Creation.

At the same time as such Divine independence is present, God also is intimately connected to human beings through the guidance -- both formally in the way of Revelation ... e.g., the Qur'an given to Muhammad, the Gospel, or Injeel, given to Jesus, the Psalms given to David, the Torah given to Moses, and the Scrolls given to Abraham (peace be upon them all), as well as informally through the Divine disclosures in relation to the internal spiritual faculties (e.g., heart and spirit) of individuals. Both forms of guidance are given for the purpose of helping human beings to come to know and understand how to take advantage of the opportunity that is inherent in created existence.

The Qur'an says:

"We have shown humankind the way, whether they be grateful or disbelieving."

The way is the process of coming to understand the truth and reality of one's existence – that is, shari'ah.

Whatever Divine qualities of majesty and rigor might be manifested toward humankind (and, I would take exception with those who are inclined to see Divine anger in everything of a problematic or catastrophic nature that occurs in relation to human beings), this has nothing to do with a failure of human beings to be obedient or committed to God – something that God does not need. Rather, whatever Divine qualities of majesty and rigor might be manifested in relation to a human being is a reflection of the complex character of the Divine challenge to which life and existence give expression.

There are many dimensions to reality. Not all of these dimensions are accessible through ease. In fact, most of them are accessible only through suffering of one kind or another.

In the end, we hurt no one but ourselves when we deny, or turn away from, the transcendent opportunity that is given expression through existence – irrespective of whether the face of such opportunity might be couched in difficulty or ease. God is concerned with human beings for our sake, not for the sake of Divinity.

The Qur'an states:

"Surely, God does no injustice to human beings, but human beings are unjust to themselves." (Surah 10, Verse 44)

Consequently, if through our own free choices, we lose out on life's opportunities, we are the ones who seal ourselves off from the knowledge and understanding that alone can help us realize our essential potential. As the Qur'an indicates:

"And whoever is blind concerning the nature of what is being revealed, will be blind in the Hereafter, and even further from the way. (Surah 17:72)

The nature of Islam, or submission, is not about obedience to a legal system or government or theological position, but, rather, submission is about a certain kind of realization concerning the nature of truth. The deeper and richer the nature of one's realization of truth is to which one has been opened, the deeper is one's submission.

Peace comes through such submission. Indeed, peace is another of the root meanings of the term "Islam".

Submission is an epistemic condition, not a condition of obedience to legal systems or laws. If one follows a particular course of action while in a condition of submission, this is because one has been brought to a state of understanding concerning the value of such a course of action, and, therefore, the character of one's behavior is rooted in the kind of understanding that one accepts as correctly reflecting the truth or reality of a given situation.

Submission is a condition of realization. Submission is a condition of accepting what has been realized. Submission is a condition that involves having one's behavior reflect what one knows and understands as a way of giving expression to one's acceptance of what has been realized. Submission is a condition of realizing, to varying degrees, important themes of understanding concerning the nature of spiritual: reality, purpose, identity, potential, and methodology.

On page 114 of *What's Right With Islam*, Imam Rauf indicates that when the term "Islam" is construed in terms of a religious system instead of a personal search for the truth concerning one's existence, the result is often sectarian chaos. I agree with him on this, but his position at this point is at odds with a great deal of what he claims elsewhere in his book, *What's Right With Islam*, and the previous pages of this essay provide considerable evidence to support my claim in this regard.

The sectarian chaos to which Imam Rauf alludes tends to arise through the behaviors of those who like to systematize and theologize spirituality in order to make what should be an individual search conform to, and comply, with a collective framework that needs to be imposed on everyone as 'the' way to God. However, there is no one way to God. There is no one way to truth or to discovering the nature of reality.

God made us as individuals. The task of life is an individual challenge with which others can assist the individual, but that challenge or task must be resolved by the person herself or himself.

Life is not meant to be an exercise in tyranny in which one group of people attempt to force other human beings to act and believe in a particular way. This is why the Qur'an stipulates that:

"There is no compulsion in the process of Deen" -- (Deen refers to process of seeking spiritual truth). (Surah 2, Verse 256).

As well, the Qur'an indicates that:

"Oppression is worse than slaughter." (Surah 2, Verse 217).

Oppression is worse than slaughter because oppression is the root cause out of which slaughter subsequently arises. Oppression is the motivational grease that lubricates the behavioral skids that run downward toward the commission of slaughter, irrespective of whether this slaughter comes to be committed by the oppressor or the oppressed.

The idea of obeying authority is really more a matter of coming to recognize and acknowledge those who are authoritative with respect to the truth of something and, then, behaving in a way that permits one to comply with the authoritativeness of such understanding ... it is not authority, per se, that one should comply with, but, rather, it is the authoritativeness of truth with which one should comply if and when such truth becomes manifest.

Not all authorities are authoritative in the foregoing sense. One should only seek to comply with the truth that comes forth through real authoritativeness.

When one is told to obey authority in the Qur'an, the guidance concerns the principle of complying with one's understanding of whatever truths might be given expression through such an authority. By obeying such authority – that is, the authoritativeness of the Qur'an, or the authoritativeness of the Prophet, or the authoritativeness of a saint, or the authoritativeness of an insight or understanding that has been given to one through a spiritual station – then under such circumstances, if one's behavior properly reflects such an understanding of the truth (and provided that one's understanding is, in fact, correct) then one is said to be obedient.

The obedience of shari'ah or Deen is always directed toward understanding and, complying with, the truth of reality. The obedience of shari'ah and Deen is not about loyalty to a government, leader, authority figure, institution, organization, state, nation, school of law, or a legal system.

God is the source of all truth. Therefore, one's obedience is to God ... and to God alone.

If, through a spiritual experience, the Prophet directly counsels one to pursue a certain course of action, then one follows such counsel. One does this because the Qur'an indicates with respect to the Prophet that he: "does not speak out of his own accord or desire." (Surah 53, Verse 3).

However people who: maintain, search through, and interpret collections of what the Prophet said more than 1400 years ago and, in the process, work out legal systems for compelling others to follow suit, such people are presuming to speak for both God and the Prophet. Moreover, they are claiming that what the Prophet said in one context more than 1400 years ago is applicable to other contexts that arise in very different historical, social, cultural, and spiritual circumstances more than 1400 years later. Such extrapolations are not only entirely unjustified, but, as well, they lead to many of the kinds of problems about which the Prophet was concerned when he told people more than 1400 years ago to not keep collections of his sayings.

The arguments that Imam Rauf seeks to put forth in relation to claiming that Muslims are under a spiritual obligation to be obedient to authority and/or the majority are, in part, based on sayings of the Prophet. To the extent that this is the case,

Imam Rauf is both presumptuous in relation to the Prophet and, as well, Imam Rauf has taken the Prophet out of the context that the latter actually was addressing.

By constructing such arguments, I believe that Imam Rauf misunderstands the actual character of shari'ah – which is for an <u>individual</u> to seek, realize, and apply the truth according to one's capacity to do so and according to the Grace bestowed on one by God to do so. Moreover, by approaching various issues as he does in his book, *What's Right With Islam*, I believe that Imam Rauf also misunderstands the nature of the kind of democracy that is inherent in: The Declaration of Independence; the Preamble to the Constitution; Article IV, Section 4 of the Constitution (which guarantees republican government to every state), and the ten amendments in the Bill of Rights ... especially, the First Amendment, as well as the Ninth and Tenth Amendment. Finally, although I believe there are some very important parallels that exist between the potential of shari'ah and the potential of inalienable rights such as "life, liberty, and the pursuit of happiness – rights that have priority over any form of government, legal system, or form of authority, just as the right to shari'ah has priority over any form of government, legal system or form of authority -- nonetheless, I believe Imam Rauf has missed the boat, so to speak, with respect to giving clarity to such parallels by failing, in many respect, to properly identify and describe the nature of those parallels ... a failing that I have attempted to rectify, to some degree, in the present essay.

81

2) Fatwa

A fatwa is a legal opinion concerning an interpretation of some dimension of shari'ah (sometimes referred to as Sacred Law) and is given by people who, supposedly, are competent to give such opinions. However, there is nothing binding upon Muslims with respect to the issuing of such an edict.

A fatwa is a legal brief. If one is persuaded by the structure of the argument and logic contained in this sort of document, then, one might use such a presentation to shape one's intention in conjunction with some spiritual problem, or other, with which one is attempting to resolve. If, alternatively, one is not persuaded by the arguments contained in such a brief, then, really, one can dismiss the document without prejudice.

In a book entitled *What is Right With Islam* by Imam Feisal Abdul Rauf, there is a fatwa that appears in an appendix. The heading for the fatwa is: "Fatwa Permitting U. S. Muslim Military Personnel to Participate in Afghanistan War Effort."

This fatwa was not written by the author of the above mentioned book. Rather, it is the collective effort of five individuals who hail from Qatar, Egypt, and Syria.

Notwithstanding the foregoing issue of authorship of the fatwa, the author of *What is Right With Islam* does mention in the main text of the book how he had recommended to *The New York Times* that it publish the fatwa. Furthermore, by not commenting on the fatwa and permitting the fatwa to stand as it is without critical or evaluative remarks, he has given his tacit endorsement to what is being said by the five framers of the aforementioned fatwa.

Ostensibly, the fatwa was generated in response to some inquiries by the "most senior chaplain of the American armed forces". Nothing was said about the circumstances under which the five authors of the fatwa were approached by the chaplain, or why these people, in particular, were consulted, or whether efforts had been made to obtain any other determination, dissenting or otherwise, in conjunction with the presenting problem.

A critical analysis of the fatwa in question is given below. This is not a counter-fatwa, but it does serve as a dissenting voice, and it encompasses a perspective that people might wish to consider when reflecting not only on the issue of whether Muslim armed services personnel should participate in wars against other Muslims, but, as well, the whole issue of what constitutes justifiable homicide in relation to people in general.

Early in the fatwa, one finds the following:

"All Muslims ought to be united against all those who terrorize the innocents, and those who permit killing of non-combatants without a justifiable reason."

The authors of the fatwa do not say what they mean by being "united", but one might offer the possibility that certain oppressive factions within the U.S. government -- both present and past -- certainly qualify as being among those to whom any person of decency would be opposed ... if in no other way than speaking out the truth in the face of tyranny.

Very serious and fundamental questions, for example, concerning legitimacy, justice, morality, and fairness could be raised about U. S. involvement in, to name but a few localities: Vietnam, Cambodia, Laos, Indonesia, the Philippines, Iran, Iraq, Africa, Palestine, and most of Latin America. If terrorizing of innocents and the killing of non-combatants without justifiable reason is the issue, then, one might want to expand one's frame of reference and think about state-sponsored terrorism in conjunction with more than just Afghanistan.

However, irrespective of who is terrorizing whom, none of this justifies killing and terrorizing innocent people during the process of tracking down criminals and apprehending them. Tens of thousands, if not hundreds of thousands, of innocents have been killed in, collectively, Afghanistan, Iraq, the Balkans, and the Sudan (when the pharmaceutical factory in Sudan was mistakenly bombed, by order of William Jefferson Clinton, as a suspected plant for producing weapons of mass destruction -- which it was proven not to be -- the one source of pharmaceuticals for Sudan was lost and, as a result, tens of thousands of innocent people died from diseases and infections for which no pharmaceuticals were available to use in treatment) -- by a self-serving, reprehensible U. S. government policy. There was no due process for any of these people to determine if there was justifiable reason as to why they should die. There was no due process to establish that such people were aiding, abetting, providing safety and comfort for, or helping to finance the perpetrators of any crimes.

Property has been destroyed in all of the foregoing instances. People have been terrorized. Innocents have been slain. International conventions have been broken. War crimes have been committed.

A rogue government has run amok on Earth. However, since this is all done behind a facade of words such as: freedom, humanitarian, liberation, justice, democracy, and rule of law, then everyone should understand that the unfortunates who have had to die, starve, become ill (through depleted uranium munitions, as well as the diseases that have been sprung loose through the systematic destruction of infrastructure), be uprooted into refugee status, and suffer -- well, this is all for a good and noble cause: U. S. hegemony in which, like ancient Greece, only the real citizens (i.e., the perpetrators of crimes) get to consent to how they are to be governed ... everyone else is mere chattel or fodder or 'deserving' of exploitation and manipulation.

The fatwa continues with:

"We find it necessary to apprehend the true perpetrators of these crimes as well as those who aid and abet them through incitement, financing or other support. They must be brought to justice in an impartial court of law."

Of course, the U. S. government does not consider the World Court to be an impartial venue of law because the Court had the audacity to find the U. S. government guilty of violating Nicaraguan sovereignty, as well as conducting illegal blockades and systematically destroying the economy and people of that country. Nor, does the U. S. government consider the United Nations an impartial court of law because the United Nations has had the temerity to seek to place constraints on how or when or if the U. S. wields its considerable military might, not to mention that the U. S. government objects to being reminded that, for almost forty years, it has been stonewalling Resolution 242 that indicates, among other things, that no country -- say Israel -- has the right to hold onto territory gained through hostilities, or that the U. S. government wishes to ignore Resolution 687 that says, among other things, that once the matter in Iraq is settled to the satisfaction of the UN Security Council -- something that is unlikely to happen because the U. S. will veto anything that is not in accordance with its plans for hegemony -- then, all weapons of mass destruction, including the nuclear weapons possessed by Israel, must be eliminated from the Middle East. The U. S. government finds such matters of international agreement inconvenient for its purposes of 'real politik', and, therefore, blames the failure of the UN on everyone but one of the real sources of difficulty that is undermining UN effectiveness -- namely, the United States government.

Now, some might wish to make the claim that the only impartial court of law is the vigilante system of the armed forces and the kangaroo courts known as military tribunals. Apparently, the only people who can be trusted are those who are infected with the same mental and spiritual disease that has been responsible for U. S. government lawlessness within the international community across many decades ... even though many truly independent people might see this as a conflict of interest with respect to basic issues of justice, fairness, and objectivity.

Really, what is the difference between what Osama and company are alleged to have done, or what the U. S. government has done, and is doing. Neither of these parties has bothered much with determining who the "true perpetrators" are. Neither of these parties has concerned themselves much with due process. Neither of these parties has given any evidence that they are concerned about whether or not the people who die, or those who are terrorized, or the property that is destroyed, or the individuals who suffer are, in fact, guilty of anything except being in the wrong place at the wrong time.

The Qur'an indicates: if even one innocent person is killed, it is as if the whole of humanity were killed. Osama – if he actually did have anything to do with 9/11

-- stands condemned by the very book that he professes allegiance.

Moreover, the Prophet Muhammad (peace be upon him) indicated that one might not wage war on the elderly, women, children, noncombatants, and one might not seek to destroy the means of livelihood of a people. And, yet, both principles of the "etiquette" of war were violated in relation both to the events of 9/11 as well as the events that unfolded subsequently to that date in relation to both Afghanistan and Iraq.

Returning to the text of the fatwa, the aforementioned legal brief seeks to address the whole problem of an individual having to differentiate the innocent from the "true perpetrators". Therefore, at a certain point, the fatwa offers a hadith of the Prophet that says:

"When two Muslims face each other in fighting and one kills the other, then both the killer and the killed are in the hell-fire. Someone said: we understand that the killer is in hell, why, then, the one who's being killed? The Prophet said: because he wanted to kill the other person."

The fatwa continues on with:

"The noble hadith mentioned above only refers to the situation where the Muslim is in charge of his affairs. He is capable of fighting or not fighting. This situation does not address the situation where a Muslim is a citizen of a state and a member of a regular army. In this case he has no choice but to follow orders."

I love the way people make things up on the fly. Unless a human being is mentally incompetent, one always is in charge of his or her affairs -- at least with respect to the choices one makes.

One choice a person has is to join, or not join, the military in the first place. One's country can be served in many ways, and being a patriot does not necessarily entail that one must kill others or destroy their property and infrastructure in order to have sincerity of commitment to the core values of the United States. Another choice one has is to choose a court martial over killing innocent people.

Alternatively, one might seek to become a conscientious objector. In other words, if, before the fact of enlistment, one were not aware of the extent to which innocent lives are terrorized and brutalized by modern warfare, then surely, when one becomes aware of this, one has a strong argument for disengaging from such activities -- an argument that is rooted in moral principle, and is not sullied by either cowardice nor a lack of love for, and patriotism toward, one's country.

Why the military would want to retain people for purposes of killing others when the hearts and souls of such people being retained are morally and spiritually not in synch with such actions, is a puzzle. Surely, the military must recognize that it takes courage to say "no" to the killing of innocents -- especially, when the military is likely to take harsh action simply because in this land of democratic freedoms, the military leadership (bold warriors that they are) feels threatened by an act of moral conscience. On the other hand, if everyone were to act in accordance with his or her moral conscience rather than submit to orders, perhaps the military might not have enough bodies to carry out the wishes of its masters in the government ... and this just won't do.

Being in charge of one's affairs does not mean one has control over the ramifications of one's choices, nor does it mean one will enjoy the consequences of one's choices. However, one always is in charge of the process of exercising one's God-given capacity to choose. This is both the strength and vulnerability of being human, and to suppose otherwise is rather shallow of the authors of the fatwa at issue.

I also would be curious as to what the reasoning is behind saying that the previous hadith, or saying of the Prophet, does not address the situation in which a Muslim is "a citizen of a state and a member of a regular army." Did the Prophet inform the authors of the fatwa that this was the case? How does one know what the scope of the Prophet's words and intentions are with respect to the cited hadith?

The fact of the matter is, we don't know. And, so, some jurists are inclined to create legal fictions in order to bridge their forays into the unknown.

In ecology there is something called: the 'precautionary principle'. This precept indicates that when one is faced with a situation in which the consequences of one's actions might lead either to foreseeable problems, or entail potential problems that our limited state of understanding is not capable of foreseeing but is capable of contemplating, then, it is better to err on the side of caution and wait until our ignorance becomes less and, as a result, we are better able to understand what is going on and what the consequences of our actions will be.

Thus, with respect to the aforementioned hadith, perhaps, it is better to err on the side of caution and entertain the possibility that the scope of the Prophet's words might actually have encompassed what the authors of the fatwa say it does not than to simply proceed, without any justification, and claim, as the authors of the fatwa do, that the hadith does not apply to Muslims who are citizens of a state and members of an army. The unsupported claim of a jurist (or even a number of them) does not take precedence over the guidance of the Prophet.

According to the authors of the fatwa, a Muslim who lives in a state where he or she is a member of a regular army:

"Has no choice but to follow orders, otherwise his allegiance and his loyalty to his country could be in doubt. This would subject him to much harm since he would not enjoy the privileges of citizenship without performing its obligations."

Aside from the fact that, as the Bible reminds us, it is better to lose the world and all its attendant privileges and allurements than it is to lose one's soul, and aside from the fact that it is better to, possibly, spend a few years in prison than to live an eternity in hell, it is unfortunate that the ideas of loyalty, allegiance, and obligations should be limited -- as the authors of the fatwa seem to indicate -- to doing what the purveyors of hegemony demand rather than to serving the principles and purposes for which the United States came into existence ... which certainly was not to embrace tyranny, injustice, immorality, and the destruction and terrorizing of innocent human beings.

We all have an absolute obligation to truth and justice. If anything, our loyalty and allegiance - - as citizens of the U. S. -- are to the principles through which the United States was conceived and not to the grotesque, sordid soiled version to which the architects of hegemony wish to call citizens. There is no virtue in enjoying the privileges of citizenship that are predicated on the death, destruction and oppression of others who are innocent.

The harm to which one is exposed through blind taqlid (unquestioning adherence) to immoral, unjust, and ill-conceived orders is not loss of the enjoyment of the privileges of citizenship, but, rather, the harm is in the loss of one's way in life. At one point in 'A Man for All Seasons' Thomas Moore is cross-examining one of the people who have committed false witness against him and Thomas Moore asks the man what the medallion is that the individual wears around his neck. The man explains that it is emblematic of being the Chancellor of Wales, to which Thomas Moore responds with: "Whereas Holy Scripture tells us that it would not profit a man if he were to gain the whole world yet were to lose his soul ... but for Wales, Richard?" Should we really encourage people to exchange the integrity and spiritual well-being of the soul for this or that worldly trinket -- no matter what the hype or glitter surrounding that trinket might be?

According to the authors of the fatwa being discussed:

"The Muslim (soldier) must perform his duty in this fight despite the feeling of uneasiness of 'fighting without discriminating'. His intentions (niyya) must be to fight for enjoining of the truth and defeating falsehood. It's to prevent aggression on the innocents, or to apprehend the perpetrators and bring them to justice. It's not his concern what other consequences of the fighting that might result in his personal discomfort since he alone can neither control nor prevent it. Furthermore, all deeds are accounted (by God) according to the intentions."

This notion that "It's not his [the soldier's] concern what other consequences of the fighting that might result in his personal discomfort" resonates all too closely with a constant refrain of the people being prosecuted at the Nuremberg trials 'I was only following orders'. One of the principles arising out of those trials and that became a precedent within modern international law is this: one cannot use the excuse of following orders to justify participating in crimes against humanity.

Furthermore, one should take issue with the contention of the authors of the fatwa that one person "alone can neither control nor prevent" such events. Each person can control and prevent his or her own participation in whatever acts are repugnant to one's moral and spiritual commitments, and, as well, are in contravention of international law.

Unfortunately, the authors of the fatwa seem to be intent on instilling a sense of learned helplessness in people. They are saying that if one individual cannot prevent such things from happening, then, one should just permit oneself to be carried along by the flow of forces and not concern oneself about such matters -- as if such matters were not encompassed by one's spiritual and moral responsibility as a human being to seek the good and avoid the evil.

Furthermore, if I am a soldier and, therefore, I know how war works -- in theory, if not in practice -- then, I know that the way modern warfare is conducted will almost certainly lead to the killing of innocents, the destruction of the property of innocent people, and the terrorizing of innocent people. Given this knowledge, how does one form the intention that one will be fighting for truth and the defeating of falsehood when the very first casualty of war is, often, truth itself.

The plans for the invasion of Afghanistan had already been drawn up prior to 9/11, and 9/11 became a convenient justification or pretext for carrying out a plan that was in the works independently of 9/11. Afghanistan is today, as it has been for hundreds of years, a critical piece of the puzzle in the game of geo-politics.

For instance, because Iran cannot be trusted by the U. S. government to do the right thing for the hegemony of the latter, the 'best' – although not the shortest -- route for the oil pipeline that has been on the drawing boards for quite some time is through Afghanistan and over to Pakistan. One of the objectives all along has been to gain control of the oil discoveries in the Caspian Sea region. The permanent military bases that are being built by the U. S. are all along the route of the proposed pipeline, and, in addition, such bases give the U. S. a ready set of staging areas to launch attacks on many places in that part of the world, that is also why the U. S. forces were being set up in, among other places, Uzbekistan. The quid pro quo of these arrangements is that Russia is given a free hand to do what it will with Chechnya and its resources -- where oppression, wholesale slaughter, and the violation of basic rights are permitted as long as they do not impact on the agenda of certain dimensions of U. S. government economic and foreign policy -- a policy that is steeped in the selfish, imperialistic, exploitive oils of hegemony with respect to the rest of the world.

How is one fighting for truth and the elimination of falsehood when one seeks to stop the Taliban but does nothing to stop the opium trade going on in Afghanistan that supplies 90% of the raw resources for the heroin that ends up on the streets of, among other places, the United States? And, ironically, the Taliban who are, for the most part, uncivilized and barbaric in their manner of rule were successful in stopping the flow of heroin into America from Afghanistan.

How is one fighting for truth and the elimination of falsehood when the vast majority of innocents outside of Kabul still live in terror and uncertainty, both because of, as well as, in spite of a U. S. military presence? How is one fighting for truth and the elimination of falsehood when the policy of the U. S. government is to protect its interests rather than the interests of the average citizen of Afghanistan, or to suppose that its interests and needs are one and the same with the needs and interests of most of the inhabitants of that country?

If God judges us according to our intentions, then, how does one expect to fare when one knows that -- propaganda aside -- one is, in many respects, not fighting for truth and the elimination of falsehood but, rather, one is fighting for the industrial-military complex's desire to control the world and its resources? Does one not have an obligation to seek for the truth with respect to what one is being told? Are there not numerous sources via the Internet, DVDs, books, magazines, and people like Chalmers Johnson, Noam Chomsky, Howard Zinn, Edward Herman, Robert McChesney, Nafeez Ahmad, Ralph Nader, Peter Montague, and others through whom to discover the evidence that discloses what is going on all around the world as well as within the United States?

Can we bury our minds and hearts in the toxic soil that is euphemistically called education in the United States and say: my intentions are pure and clear? Does God not see every little fleeting bit of evidence that we allow to slip through our consciousness unchallenged that suggests that the truth is something other than what we are being asked to digest as the "official" line on things?

Niyat, or intention, is not something that forms in a vacuum. It is rooted in experience, and when the heart plays fast and loose with the truth of experience, then no matter what the superficial form of the intention might be, there is sub-text that flows in our heart of hearts and something of the truth registers with us ... and it is this that is our true intention rather than that which is given for public consumption, and it is this for which we will be held accountable.

The authors of the fatwa in question maintain:

"Muslim jurists have ruled that what a Muslim cannot control he cannot be held accountable for, as God (the Most High) says: "And keep your duty to God as much as you can" [64:16]. The Prophet (prayer and

peace be upon him) said: "When I ask of you to do
something, do it as much as you can."

One's duty to God does not consist in enabling the military-industrial complex to acquire hegemony over the world. One's duty to God does not consist in killing innocent people, destroying their property, or terrorizing non-combatants.

In addition, the Prophet hasn't asked one to do any of these things either. So, contrary to what the authors of the fatwa are suggesting, we are not obligated to do as much of these things as we can.

Moreover, one might ask the question: what does 'doing as much as one can' entail? Isn't it ironic that in a country that claims it is democratic and based upon principles of justice, fairness, truth, and liberty, one is not free to exercise one's conscience, in the matter of war, without running the risk of suffering considerable punitive damages. Yet, irrespective of whatever these damages might be, just as one is prepared to risk hardship in battle, one should be prepared to risk hardship in the cause of truth and justice.

This is what we can do. This is an essential part of what it means to be a human being.

The aforementioned fatwa says:

"Even if fighting causes him discomfort spiritually or psychologically, this personal hardship must be endured for the greater public good, as the jurisprudence (fiqh) rule states."

And, how does one calculate the greater public good? What values does one use? What methods does one apply? What criteria are to be consulted?

According to the fatwa, "the Muslim here" -- that is, the one who is a soldier:

"Is part of a whole, if he absconds, his departure will result in great harm, not only for him but for the Muslim community in his country -- and here there are many millions of them."

What is this "great harm" that will accrue to the soldier of conscience and his community? Very little is said in this regard, but mention is made that if a person does not sell his or her soul to the military-industrial complex, then it could be that the allegiance and loyalty of Muslims will come into doubt.

Allegiance and loyalty to what: To someone's warped way of dealing with the world? To someone's burning greed? To someone's indifference to the suffering of innocent people who are in the way of some geo-political objective? To someone's desire to proceed through life in an immoral, illegal way that violates the norms of decency that have been established by many countries and many billions of people?

Are the authors of the fatwa suggesting that in order not to have to deal with the unpleasantness of someone having doubts about where one's loyalties and allegiance lie, that one should betray the ideals of the Declaration of Independence and the Constitution -- not to mention, one's relationship with God and the truth? Is it really okay to destroy innocent people by the thousands, to destroy their property, to destroy their means of livelihood, so that Muslims in America won't have to deal with someone questioning their loyalty and allegiance? Is this the greater good?

The authors of the fatwa go on to say:

"The questioner [a Muslim military chaplain] inquires about the possibility of the Muslim military personnel in the American armed forces to serve in the back lines -- such as in the relief services sector and similar works. If such requests are granted by the authorities, without reservation or harm, to the soldiers, or to other American Muslim citizens, then, they should request that. Otherwise, if such a request: raises doubts about their allegiance or loyalty, casts suspicions, presents them with false accusations, harms their future careers, sheds misgivings on their patriotism, or similar sentiments, then it is not permissible to ask for that."

Who and what is necessitating that it is not permissible to make such a request? Is it God? Is it the Prophet? Well, actually, it isn't. It is a group of five jurists who are saying this is impermissible. Moreover, they are saying it is impermissible on the basis of dubious interpretations of what the Qur'an and hadith have said.

And, why are they saying it is impermissible? Well, as everyone knows, the threat of harsh words, suspicions, doubts, false accusations, future careers, and the like are far more important than a few thousand lives over in Afghanistan. This is the calculus of the jurisprudence of the five people who have authored the fatwa in question.

Whether the lives of the innocent people in Afghanistan whose lives will be destroyed by a U. S. invasion are Muslim or not Muslim is immaterial. The Qur'an does <u>not</u> say: 'if anyone killed a Muslim human being - unless it be in punishment for murder or for spreading mischief on earth -- it would be as though he killed all of humanity'. The Qur'an states the prohibition against killing without qualification as far as the identity, race, ethnicity, gender, religion, or beliefs of the individual being killed are concerned.

The fatwa being examined here ends with:

"This is in accordance with the Islamic jurisprudence rules which state that necessities dictate exceptions, as well as the rule which says that one might endure a small harm to avoid a much greater harm."

The authors have stated things incorrectly by claiming that the principles of jurisprudence that they consider to be applicable actually demand what they are claiming.

First, the much greater harm in the issue before the authors of the fatwa is the killing of innocent people rather than not having to endure the suspicions, doubts and false accusations of others concerning one's loyalty, allegiance, duty, and patriotism that they have identified as the greater harm. In addition, the greater harm is in enabling Muslims to kill others -- whether those other human beings are Muslim or non-Muslim -- without just cause and due process and just because someone who has a hidden agenda says they should.

Secondly, the principle that "necessities dictate exceptions" presupposes that it is necessary to kill innocent human beings, and the authors of the fatwa have not established this, nor will they ever be able to establish this. The killing of innocent human beings is never necessary except in the schemes and machinations of those who lust after what does not belong to them and who have a pathological need to control the rest of the world.

3) Openings

While I share some of the goals that are espoused in *What's Right With Islam* by Imam Feisal Abdul Rauf -- namely, its ecumenical spirit, as well as its emphasis on such qualities as: peace, liberty, harmony, justice, democracy, plurality, and moral reciprocity -- nevertheless, there seem to be a number of issues that are relevant to the realization of such goals, yet, which are not actually rigorously pursued in Imam Rauf's book, or if they are engaged, this seems to be done in ways that are of questionable persuasiveness, if not tenability.

The construction of a logical argument can be a complex, layered, nuanced process. Often times, this is the purpose of writing a book -- to devote the time, space, and effort necessary to develop, in as persuasive a manner as possible (at least in principle) the essential features of a perspective together with the reasons, demonstrations, proofs, and so on that might assist other individuals to not only understand the world of discourse as one does, but, as well, to agree with what is being said.

Such arguments build on ideas both little and large. The dynamics of such ideas that are expressed through the inner structure of a work, form the woof and warp through which the horizon and foci of a discourse are woven. A lot of little things can matter as much as one large issue. Each informs, shapes, and colors the other. Consequently, the validity of each is often caught up with the logical character of the others.

The following analysis examines some of the little and large aspects of *What's Right With Islam*. This critical exploration is not exhaustive with respect to all that might have been discussed in conjunction with the aforementioned book, but I believe the reader will get the gist or drift of where I stand in relation to much of what is contained with Imam Rauf's book.

On page xviii of the Preface, one finds the following statement:

"The U. S. military victory over Saddam Hussein's regime in Iraq means that America is now responsible for shaping a new Iraq."

The foregoing assertion presumes much and evades even more. One can think of a lot of possibilities that might have been said -- perhaps, should have been said -- in the foregoing observation rather than what was said. For example, one might have said: America is now morally responsible for re-building the infrastructure of Iraq at its (the U. S.'s) own expense; or, America is now morally responsible for paying indemnity to the tens of thousands of innocent families who lost loved ones as a result of the actions of the U. S. government but who had nothing to do with Saddam Hussein's regime; or, America is now legally and morally responsible for leaving Iraq and permitting Iraqis to shape their own destiny.

One has trouble understanding how a war that was predicated on lie after lie, and falsehood after falsehood, or that was conducted in violation of international law, and that was undertaken without legal authority to do so gives one any morally sanctioned responsibility to shape another country and people. Invading another country because one wishes to do so, or because it serves one's imperial designs or desire for hegemony, does not constitute legal authority. After all, if one might wage war simply because of unjustified desires, then, Nazi Germany had legal authority to invade Czechoslovakia and Poland, or the former Soviet Union had legal authority to invade Hungary, and so on.

Moreover, while Saddam Hussein and most of the rest of his pack of jokers might have been apprehended, any talk of victory in the foregoing quote is rather premature. A "victory" that entails, collectively, thousands of additional dead and in which it is not safe to walk the streets or go about life in a normal fashion is not like any victory I have ever heard of - - except, of course, that of a Pyrrhic victory that some might say is a euphemism for the fact that much more is at stake in Iraq than a PR banner hanging from the upper decks of an aircraft carrier somewhere off the coast of San Diego, far from the realities of what was transpiring in Iraq. A "victory" that stands a very good chance of, sooner or later, inducing Iraq to slide into a civil war is not much of a victory -- except to those who want some sort of trophy to mount on the walls of their war room and who are not really all that concerned about what happens to the millions of innocents who have been placed in harm's way by the actions of the U. S. government.

Whatever the sins of Saddam Hussein might have been -- and they were many -- there are three things that need to be kept in mind. First, almost all of his sins were aided, abetted and subsidized by the United States government across a number of administrations, both Republican and Democrat. Secondly, it is an oxymoron to suppose one can generate democracy by fiat or through brutal oppression -- and this is as true for the United States as it was for Saddam Hussein. And, finally, the oil resources in Iraq do not belong to the West, or to Saddam Hussein, or to whomever else forms the government there, or to this or that corporation ... those resources belong to the Iraqi people -- all of them ... anything else is theft no matter what the contractual and legal euphemisms might read.

Imam Rauf goes on to liken what the U. S. military has done, and must do, in Iraq as falling under the rubric of a saying of Prophet Muhammad (peace be upon him) concerning the distinction between the lesser and greater jihad. According to Imam Rauf:

"America has now won the lesser jihad, that of toppling the Saddam regime."

Something can be a jihad only if it is in compliance with divinely established conditions of morality. There is nothing about the U. S. invasion of Iraq that is moral.

Even the pretext of liberating Iraq is an ethical farce because the forces within the Executive Branch, the Pentagon, and among the leading defense contractors who were architects of this tragedy never had any intention of really permitting the Iraqi people to have self-determination. As has happened so many times before in U. S. history when the U. S. wants a regime change somewhere (e.g., Noriega in Panama, Allende in Chile, Mossadegh in Iran), the central, motivating factor is that whomever is to be removed is someone who is refusing to comply with, or creating problems for, U. S. plans for economic and political hegemony in some given part of the world.

The U. S. government wants a tyrant in Iraq. But, they want their kind of tyrant -- someone who would be in harmony with U. S. interests, and the people of Iraq be dammed.

As long as Saddam served U. S. purposes (e.g., waging war against Iran), then, Saddam was 'the man' and he was given wide latitude to amuse himself with the lives of the Iraqi people as he desired. When he stopped serving the purposes of U. S. hegemony and became too big a liability, the U. S. government (or, at least, certain elements within that government) began to plan for a regime change -- not for the purpose of establishing democracy, but for the purpose of arranging for a new government that would be subservient to the interests of the cartel that is now, and has been for quite some time, running the U. S. government (Dwight Eisenhower knew very well what he was talking about when, nearly fifty years ago, he warned the people of the United States about the military-industrial complex that was undermining democracy in the United States.).

It is a travesty of all that the Prophet Muhammad (peace be upon him) taught and lived to try to claim that what the U. S. has done, and is doing, in Iraq is a lesser jihad, even remotely similar to anything in which the Prophet participated. Among other things, indiscriminate killing, injustice, wholesale destruction of a society's infrastructure and brutal oppression have no place in even a jihad of a lesser kind.

Imam Rauf goes on to say:

"Its (the U. S.'s) larger challenge lies ahead; winning the hearts and minds of Iraqis, and through them, the rest of the Muslim world. This waging of peace is now America's greater jihad."

The greater jihad is about purification of oneself. Before -- if ever -- one seeks to try to tell others how they ought to live their lives, one should put one's own house in order. Otherwise, at the very least, one is guilty of sheer hypocrisy.

If the U. S. government were really interested in waging peace, they never would have begun any of the wars -- not under Bush II, and not under Clinton, and not under Bush I. If the U. S. wants to win the hearts and minds of the Iraqis, then, it should stop killing them, oppressing them, destroying their means of livelihood, and interfering with their country.

The U. S. government is not capable of truly assisting other countries until it cleanses itself of its imperial ambitions. Until the U. S. government stops seeking to control the people of other countries (via corrupt, tyrannical governments) or refrains from exploiting those people and cheating them (via dealings with corrupt, tyrannical governments), any mention of the 'greater jihad' in conjunction with U. S. policy is nothing but a charade that misdirects attention away from the actual, insidious activities of the U. S. government and its corporate buddies.

Just as the desire for anything beyond the struggle for truth sullies the idea of the greater jihad in relation to individuals, so too, the desire for anything beyond the struggle to live in accordance with truth taints the intentions of the U. S. government. One can't lust after the resources of another country and, simultaneously, claim that one is merely engaging in the greater jihad. One can't dream of exploiting another people and say, with any sincerity, that one's actions are those of the greater jihad.

The greater jihad for the U. S. government has nothing to do with winning the hearts of the Iraqi people or the rest of the Muslim world. The challenge facing the U. S. government is not waging peace in the world, but to purify its own political house and, thereby, liberate America from the stranglehold that bad government and large corporations have had on the American people.

If, God willing, the U. S. government is capable of accomplishing this process of self-purification, then, in many ways, world peace will follow naturally. After all, if the United States government (or the corporations it sponsors and subsidizes) is not marauding about and interfering in, oppressing, terrorizing, undermining, and destroying the lives of other peoples, then, many (although, regrettably, not all) of the causes of conflict in the world would disappear. Unfortunately, so far, the U. S. government has had neither the honesty nor the insight of an old Walt Kelly comic strip called "Pogo" in which one of the characters utters the line: "We have met the enemy, and they is us."

On page xxi of *What's Right With Islam*, Imam Rauf says:

"...continuing news of suicide bombers in Israel, and in Muslim countries such as Pakistan, Indonesia, and Iraq, and more recently in Saudi Arabia and Morocco, have further reinforced American stereotypes about and fear of Muslims.

"Fear breeds a number of things: hatred of anything associated with 'the enemy' -- from ethnic appearance to clothing and religion - and a circling-of-the-wagons mentality. This country veered uncritically to the right."

America did not just veer to the right. It was maneuvered in that direction. The generation of an atmosphere of fear has always been one of the main weapons of choice to use to whip the public into a state of compliancy with respect to the wishes of those who are in charge.

In the light of substantial historical evidence, such words and phrases as: "Remember the Maine", the U.S.S Lusitania, Pearl Harbor, the Gulf of Tonkin, the drug lord Noriega, the innocent college students at risk in Grenada, April Glaspie, the slaughter of the incubator babies in Kuwait, satellite photos allegedly showing Saddam about to attack Saudi Arabia, and weapons of mass destruction -- all of these incidents have been shown to carry suspect pedigrees concerning the validation of events being what they were portrayed to be by the U. S. government and its media outlets. In each of the foregoing cases, elements within the United States government have been implicated, either directly or indirectly, as helping to arrange for the perpetration of tragedies that enrage the people of the U. S. and help render the latter target group more supple for purposes of further government manipulation.

Similar evidence exists with respect to the 9/11 attacks. If one doubts this, then, you might want to read *The War On Truth* by Nafeez Mossaddeq Ahmed in which considerable evidence is put forth about how and why the United States was attacked in 2001 by alleged remnants of al-Qaida. As the foregoing book points out, one of the scandals of the 9/11 Commission is that it never really explored important aspects of the relevant, available evidence. There were vast areas of essential data that were either ignored or glossed over by the Commission, and there were a number of fundamental questions that were never raised by it in any rigorous fashion, if at all.

Michael Moore's *Fahrenheit 9/11* has a lot of fun with the seven to ten minutes of inaction when President Bush sat in a Florida classroom listening to children read about a pet goat rather than politely excusing himself and responding to the information he had been given about ongoing events in the air. The fact of the matter is, however, news reports indicate President Bush knew about the hijackings <u>before</u> he ever went into the grade school classroom, and, so, the question that Michael Moore omitted is why didn't the President do anything about the situation <u>before</u> he went into the classroom?

With certain exceptions, only the President can give the order for commercial air planes to be shot down. Without a doubt, having to make a decision about whether to destroy innocent lives aboard those commercials flights rather than risk the potential of even greater loss of innocent lives on the ground would be a terrible burden for any human being.

However, if someone can give the order to attack Afghanistan with the understanding that innocent lives will be lost, and if someone can give the order to attack Iraq with the clear understanding that innocent lives will be lost, then, perhaps, someone should have been ready to make a decision that would have made subsequent decisions to attack Afghanistan and Iraq less easy than they appeared to be.

There might, or might not, be entirely reasonable answers for all of these questions. However, one won't know any of this one way or the other until all of this is given a rigorous public airing and critical scrutiny -- something the media has not done to date, nor, as far as I can see, has the 9/11 Commission properly addressed ... unless they did so behind closed doors and feel the U. S. public has no right to know about issues that directly affect our lives, our sense of security, or our confidence in the integrity of government.

The foregoing is not an effort to foment conspiracy theories. Rather, it is intended to induce people to question the version of events that is put forth by authority.

Time and time again, people in authority have proven themselves unworthy of the trust of the people. In fact, due to the sheer quantity of prevarications on the part of all too many government officials for all too many years, the general operating procedure of the public should be that anything the government says should be handled through HAZMAT protective gear until one can establish that the information is not toxic or hazardous to one's health.

Just because some government employee or elected official offers an "official" version of events, this doesn't mean the 'official version' is a true reflection of what actually happened. It might only mean that this sort of 'official version' is what such government figures want the public to believe in order to advance ulterior, illicit machinations of their own.

None of the foregoing is to suggest that the terrible things that were transpiring in Muslim countries were not taking place, or that there were no reasons for a prudent person to be fearful about how events were spinning out of control almost everywhere. However, such events were only part of what is going on, and there is much need for something akin to when Paul Harvey says: "And, now, the rest of the story", for much has been kept from the eyes, minds, and hearts of the American people by its own government officials ... not just with respect to 9/11 but with respect to several hundred years of history.

I agree with Imam Rauf when he says, in relation to the aforementioned reactionary 'move to the right' of America, that it was largely uncritical (at least among large sections of the public, much of the media, and most of the politicians). However, there were many forces in play that were designed to shield events from the probing, curious eye of critical reflection, and, therefore, it was not just happenstance that events were ushered toward the right in an uncritical fashion ... there was a conscious intentionality guiding this move rightward into a reactionary state of fear.

In conjunction with the foregoing, Imam Rauf raises the question:

"Was Samuel Huntington right? Were we witnessing a 'clash of civilizations' between the West and the rest - in this case between Western civilization and Islam?"

The short answer is 'no'.

What we were witnessing (which requires a much longer answer) were a series of staged events, or predictable reactions to staged events, that were designed to frame the understanding of the public in certain ways. The purpose of these attempts to frame people's perception of reality was to enable various parties to have a pretext of justification, and/or plausible deniability, with respect to seeking to organize the world according to an agenda of hegemony -- and this is as true for the fundamentalist religious zealots as it is for the fundamentalist capitalistic and military zealots, both of whom seek to seduce their respective spheres of influence like a cat in heat.

According to Imam Rauf, the events of 9/11 changed him and his life.

"I went from refusing to get dragged into politics because I saw it as a no-win situation to being forced to explain myself and defend my faith."

Unlike the author of *What's Right With Islam*, I do not feel the need to explain myself or defend my faith. With respect to the latter matter, my faith is precisely that: 'my faith', and as such, it is not something that I have to defend to others.

Of course, Imam Rauf might have meant that he felt the need to defend Islam, but Islam does not need any defense. It is what it is, and God defends it very well -- which is why, among other things, there has been a long tradition of Prophets, some 125,000 individuals long, who have been sent to human beings in order to help people understand the nature of spirituality and why, as well, there have been a number of Books of Revelation that were issued down through the ages.

Furthermore, I do not feel the need to explain myself to anyone. I didn't fly those planes on September 11, 1991, I am not a member of al-Qaida nor do I support or endorse their activities, nor have I done anything to either subvert the Constitution of the United States, nor have I tried to exploit the peoples of other lands or interfere with their lives.

Several decades before 9/11 ever occurred, I chose not to participate in U. S. aggression against other peoples. I do not now countenance acts of aggression against the United States – whoever might be responsible for such acts.

The exercise of violence solves very few, if any, problems. In general, and with the possible exception of defending one's home or country against armed invasion, I tend to agree with the sentiments of Issac Asimov as expressed in his <u>Foundation</u> series when one of his characters says: "Violence is the last refuge of incompetence."

In addition, for more than thirty years, I have been actively engaged in striving for truth in matters of: spirituality, justice, equality, freedom, peace, and human rights, in conjunction with governments, universities, the media, Muslims, and non-Muslims.

Hostility and anger toward Muslims did not suddenly erupt on September 1, 2001. I can remember in 1967 when I was working in the student center cafeteria at MIT.

The television was carrying news coverage of the 1967 war between Israel and some of its Arab neighbors. With each advance and victory of the Israeli army, there was much cheering and jubilation that took place in the room where the television was, and as well, there was much jeering and contempt toward the Arabs and Muslims.

I was not a Muslim at the time, and I was not partial to either side. However, I do remember that hostility, contempt, and anger that were present and directed toward Arabs and Muslims.

During half of the 1970s and for much of the 1980s, I experienced, first hand, as a recent convert to Islam, the deep-rooted suspicion, enmity, and ignorance that existed in many parts of the West with respect to Muslims and Islam. More specifically, as a member of a Muslim organization that published a report that was critical of the offensive and inaccurate material concerning Islam and the Prophet Muhammad (peace be upon him) that appeared in a number of school textbooks being used in the public school systems in the Province of Ontario, I went round and round the barn with all manner of alleged intellectuals, media types, and government officials about the many facets of prejudice.

During this period of time I received a remarkable education concerning the underbelly of Western 'civilization'. I discovered there were many so-called experts of Islamic Studies who preferred error to accuracy and who were quite indignant that anyone should object to the way in which their lack of understanding and personal animosities or special interests would be used to validate ignorance. I encountered representatives of the media who believed it was their God-given duty to perpetuate ignorance and bias concerning Muslims and Islam. I negotiated with government officials who did what such individuals often tend to do best: evade, procrastinate, stonewall, lie, and manipulate.

I remember an instance in which a group of people from a local mosque were lodging an official complaint with a business in the community. The group had asked me to be its spokesperson.

When we were ushered into the office of the manager of the business with which we were concerned, the manager looked at me, and, then, he looked at the others (who were from Pakistan, Africa, India, and the like), and, then, he looked back at me. He whispered to me -- because I was the person closest to him: "I know what they are doing here, but what are you doing here." I pointed over to the group of people with whom I arrived and whispered back: "I'm one of them."

Alternatively, I also recall a number of instances when Muslims actively voiced their hostility toward me and resented my presence because my skin color and linguistic pedigree were not to their liking. So, prejudice and bias are not the exclusive preserves of non-Muslims.

In the early 1980's, Sheik Ahmad Zaki Yamani, the Minister of Oil for Saudi Arabia, came to Canada. My Sufi shaykh sought a meeting with Sheik Yamani in an attempt to get support from him with respect to some of the textbook bias work we were doing as well as in relation to a number of other matters.

My spiritual guide didn't think we had much of a chance of meeting with the extremely busy minister, but my shaykh thought: 'nothing ventured, nothing gained'. To his surprise, we received a call back from the person managing appointments for the oil Sheik and said we had been granted a five minute audience with the Oil Minister on such and such day.

When we went for our appointment, the RCMP and Canadian officials who were present (but outside the room where Sheik Yamani was receiving people) were quite curious about just who we were and why we were seeing the Saudi Oil Minister. What was scheduled for five minutes turned into a meeting that lasted more than an hour. Whatever curiosity the Canadian authorities had prior to our meeting with the Sheik was quadrupled, or more, by the time our meeting was through.

It turned out that the Oil Minister was, and is, a great lover of the Prophet Muhammad (peace be upon him). When he discovered that we also were lovers of the Prophet, then all formalities, time constraints, and official distance that might have been between us disappeared.

While he served each of us (there were four of us) tea in a very humble and attentive way, he talked about his family, some of the miraculous things that had happened to him, and much more. He invited members of the group to visit with him in Saudi Arabia as his guests, all expenses paid. He gave each of us a personal gift of some kind.

As Saudi Oil Minister and one of the leading strategists of OPEC's 1973 price hike, he easily could have destroyed the West if he wanted to do so. He was not interested in doing that -- rather, he simply wanted international economic arrangements that would establish as much distributive justice as possible for all parties concerned -- Muslim and non-Muslim.

When the price hike came, people in the West were outraged with the OPEC countries. What right did OPEC have to do this?

These same people who were complaining would think nothing about mouthing the platitude of the law of supply and demand if they stood to benefit from the scarcity of a non-renewable resource. Moreover, these same people would lose absolutely no sleep over the hardships placed on nations through the economic restructuring pressures imposed by the World Bank or the International Monetary Fund as conditions for getting loans, and, yet, these same people would howl in outrage when the quality of their lives was adversely affected due to the pressures of economic restructuring caused by the action of others -- such as OPEC.

The events that ensued from 9/11 in relation to hostility toward, and hatred of, Muslims and Islam was more of the same of what has been going on for a long, long time. The only difference was that now Americans had been killed or were suffering, directly, or indirectly, as a result of the attacks, and, perhaps, for the very first time, Americans, as a people, had some visceral insight into how Muslims in other parts of the world have been feeling for several hundred years as imperial powers from the West killed, pillaged, plundered and raped their countries and peoples.

That people died in the World Trade Towers, the Pentagon, and in a field in Pennsylvania gives expression to a great injustice against those innocent individuals. But, the people of America should get a grip on themselves and garner a little historical perspective for such things have been happening with great regularity all over the world and our government is not innocent in such matters.

The fact that much of the American public is ignorant about these kinds of issues (and intentionally kept that way for the most part) does not mean that similar, if not worse, tragedies have not been occurring elsewhere in the world. If someone screams in pain and no one hears it or pays attention to it, the fact of the matter is that the person who screams still feels pain.

If anyone needs to explain themselves it is the U. S. government and all of those Muslim governments who have aided and abetted U. S. and Western imperial aims. If anyone needs to explain themselves it is the so-called democratic countries that have bequeathed something other than democracy to its citizens. If there is anyone who needs to explain themselves, it is all the so-called Muslim leaders who have betrayed Islam and their compatriots by establishing something other than peaceful conditions in which a person's pursuit of Islam can prosper without compulsion and oppression. If there is something that is demanded of the present situation it is for a resolute intention among all human beings to seek, as much as possible, the truth of things and not be satisfied with the shoddy, self-serving "official" offerings of this or that government.

4) The Two Commandments

According to Imam Rauf in his book *What's Right With Islam*, there are at least two core values that are shared by America and Islam. First, both accept the principle that one should love God with all one's soul, heart, strength, and mind. Secondly, each endorses the value of loving one's neighbor, as one loves oneself.

While on the level of ideals, there might be some truth to the foregoing contention, nevertheless, in practice, one might raise considerable doubt as to the degree to which either Americans or Muslims actually seek to live in accordance with such ideals. Neither Americans nor Muslim are, on the whole, what they once were or might have become.

There is a reason why the Prophet Muhammad (peace be upon him) indicated that if those who enjoyed the company of the Prophet were to leave out even one-tenth of what was obligatory upon them, they would face severe, spiritual consequences, but, nonetheless, there would come a time when if a people -- who had not seen the Prophet -- were to do even one-tenth of what was obligatory upon them, then such people would, nonetheless, achieve Paradise. Spiritually speaking, on average, people are getting worse, not better, and the ramifications of such spiritual illnesses are reflected in the events of the world, both locally and as a whole.

To be sure, one comes across instances of humanity among both Americans and Muslims who are bright beacons of spiritual expression and living embodiments of the aforementioned ideals, but, unfortunately, this does not occur with anywhere near the frequency of what might have been the case in the past. In fact, there is often considerable disagreement among people with respect to just what it means to, for example, love God with all one's soul, heart, strength and mind.

Moreover, one might also have reservations about being loved by someone else as they love themselves because, perhaps, one might not be enamored with the manner in which such people love themselves. One might feel more comfortable with having others do unto one as such people would have one do unto them.

Isn't: 'loving one's neighbor as one loves oneself' the same thing as: 'do unto others as one would have others do unto you'? Not necessarily.

Suppose I live my life in accordance with a particular theology, and let us further suppose that I really love this theology along with all that I believe it has done for my life. Now, if I follow the principle that I should love my neighbor as I love myself, then I am going to want my neighbor to love this theology that I am loving for myself ... and, thus, is born the evangelical spirit that is at the heart of a lot of problems in the world, both with respect to Americans and Muslims.

If, on the other hand, I adopt the principle that I should try to do unto others as I would have others do unto me, then my approach to things might be quite different. More specifically, since I would not necessarily like someone coming into my life trying to foist onto me what they love for themselves, I might be somewhat cautious about what I try to impose on such an individual, knowing that I am attempting to establish a precedent through my behavior that creates an invitation for the other person to interact with me as I am interacting with them -- namely, if I don't seek to proselytize in relation to you, please don't proselytize with respect to me.

So, whether, or not, I want someone to love me as they love themselves really depends on how they love themselves. There are quite a few ways of loving oneself with respect to which I would just as soon take a pass.

However, I can think of no exceptions to the principle of reciprocity that is at the heart of the Golden Rule. "So in everything, do to others what you would have them do to you, for this sums up the Law and the Prophets." (Matthew 7:12)

If I do not wish to be oppressed and exploited by others, then I should not seek to oppress or exploit such individuals. If I wish to be treated with justice, then I should endeavor to do justice to others. If I do not wish to be hungry, then I should be willing to feed others. If I do not wish to be deprived of my livelihood, then I should try to not deprive others of their livelihood. If I do not wish to be killed or harmed, then I should strive not to kill or harm other people. If I wish to be forgiven for the injustices and unkindness that I have perpetrated against others, then I need to entertain the idea of working on forgiving those who have done injustice to me.

If I do not treat others as I would want to be treated, then it should come as no surprise to me if others should follow my lead and treat me as I have treated them. Extraordinary strength of character is required not to offer tit for tat, that, unfortunately, is the road most traveled by the majority of us. Life lived in accordance with the Golden Rule is clean, simple, and straightforward -- although doing so does require some integrity for which we must struggle. Life lived in accordance with the hypocrisy of wanting to be treated one way, but doing the opposite in relation to other people, tends to be a very messy affair that explains, perhaps, why the world is such a mess.

Thus, there are two kinds of reciprocity. One kind leads, God willing, to felicity, while the other form of reciprocity leads to nothing but difficulty and heartache.

The former kind is the more difficult path to pursue, but it leads, God willing, to ease. The latter form of reciprocity is born in the ease of giving expression to the natural inclinations of the

unredeemed soul, but it ends, always, in difficulty --
unless God wishes otherwise.

According to Imam Rauf, Muslims tend to fulfill this second commandment -- that is, to love one's neighbor as one's self -- through a strong sense of valuing the community over individualism, as well as by means of seeking to instill a deep-rooted sense of feeling a responsibility toward others, including through charitable acts. There is a great deal of wealth in the Muslim world, and there is a great deal of poverty, and, so, a natural question to ask is this: if what Imam Rauf says is true, then why are the two aforementioned facts concerning the Muslim world simultaneously true?

Is one to conclude that the extent of poverty just overwhelms the capacity of rich Muslims who are being as generous as they can be? Or, does the answer to the foregoing question lie in another direction?

The Qur'an says:

"And, they ask thee (O Muhammad) what they ought to spend (in the way of God). Say: that which is left after meeting your needs." (Qur'an, 2:219)

But, how many Muslims -- rich or otherwise -- actually adhere to this teaching? More often than not, they seek the advice of some of the kissing cousins of the accountants for Enron, WorldCom, and others who are morally challenged, to help the wealthy make every luxury on which they spend money a "need" so that they will be free of any obligation to their fellow human beings, just as all too many very wealthy corporations often find ways not to have to pay any income tax.

There is a related idea in the Bible when Jesus (peace be upon him) says:

"It is easier for a camel to go through the eye of a needle than for a rich man to enter the kingdom of God." (Mark 10:25)

How many Christians believe that the Bible is the literal word of God, and, yet, hold on to their wealth as if the above words of Jesus (peace be upon him) had never been uttered?

Furthermore, to suppose, as Imam Rauf seems to indicate on page 2 of his book, that Islam favors community over the individual seems, at the very least, rather a questionable contention. Islam indicates that both community and individuals should strive to be in harmony with one another, but this is a matter of balance not of preferring one to the other, since both the community and individuals have responsibilities, one to the other.

In addition, the issue of charity is not a matter of favoring the community over the individual but of making sure that the community has the means of looking after, and helping, those individuals who are in need. Charity is an individual responsibility that, aside from being one of the pillars of deen, is also an expression of one individual's compassion for, and empathy with, other individuals. Helping others is an individual responsibility that has communal ramifications, and is not a statement about the priority of community over the individual.

Individualism that is an expression of nafsi amarrah (the unredeemed, carnal soul) is not acceptable within Islam, but this has nothing to do with the priority of community over the individual. Instead, this is an acknowledgment of the damage to others that the unredeemed nafs can do.

Individualism that is an expression of the unique gifts that God has bequeathed upon a human being is one of the resources of a community and, as such, should be both protected and encouraged so that, God willing, its inherent potential might be realized for the benefit of all -- including the individual. All a person has to contribute is who, in essence, she or he is, and this is nothing other than our individuality that -- when that locus is properly purified, calibrated, and activated -- can serve as a locus of manifestation through which Divine Grace shines.

With respect to this potential of the individual, one has an obligation before God, and, as well, one owes a duty of care both to oneself and to others -- individually and collectively -- to struggle to fulfill one's most essential nature or fitra. To state the foregoing, however, is a very different proposition than to claim that the community has priority over, or should be valued more than, the individual, as Imam Rauf seems to be claiming is the case in the Muslim world -- in fact, to whatever extent this claim is the norm, it might constitute a distortion of the principles of Islam.

In *What's Right With Islam*, Imam Rauf states he believes that what Muslims do right is to observe the first commandment -- that is, through observance of the five pillars, Muslims, he feels, fulfill the requirements of loving God with all their soul, heart, mind, and strength. Aside from the problem of trying to determine just how observant Muslims are with respect to the five pillars -- and I think it is presumptuous and foolhardy to offer self-congratulations before the results of the Day of Judgment have been announced -- one might note, as well, that reducing the idea of 'loving God with all one's soul, heart, mind, and strength' down to the five pillars might also be problematic.

The term 'love' is used very loosely these days by all too many people. What is love?

Shaykh al-Shibli (may Allah be pleased with him) says that love:

"Is like a cup of fire which blazes terribly; when it takes root in the senses and settles in the heart, it annihilates."

Hazrat Muin-ud-din Chishti (may Allah be pleased with him) concurs with the Shaykh when Khawaja Sahib says that:

"The heart of one devoted to God is a fire place of love; whatever comes into it is burnt and becomes annihilated."

Hazrat Ra'bia of Basra (may Allah be pleased with her) resonates with the same essential principle of love when she prays:

"Oh, Allah, if I worship Thee out of desire of Heaven, then, deny me Heaven, and if I worship Thee out of fear of Hell, then, throw me into Hell, but if I worship Thee for Thee and Thee alone, then, grant me Thy vision".

In addition, there is a tradition told among the Sufis that says:

"God indicates that the souls of humankind were loving Him, and, then, they were shown the world, and 9/10ths of humankind forget about God and became immersed in the world. Then, the remaining 1/10th who are still loving God were shown the delights of Paradise, and 9/10ths of these souls forgot about God and became preoccupied with Paradise. Of the 1/10th who are left, still loving God, difficulties are showered on them, and, as a result, 9/10ths of these individuals ran away from God. Of the 1/10th of 1/10th of 1/10th of the original population who still remain, God tells them that He will visit such tribulations upon them that they will be crushed, and these souls responded: "As long as it is from Thee Oh Lord."

All of the foregoing is rooted firmly in a Hadith Qudsi that says:

"Whoever seeks Me, finds Me; whoever finds Me, comes to know Me; whoever comes to know Me, loves Me; whoever loves Me, that person I slay; whomever I slay, I owe that person blood-money, and to whomever I owe blood-money, I am the recompense for that blood-money."

Clearly, the one who loves God is slain in the fire of annihilation, known as fana, in which nothing but the Reality of Divinity fills the awareness of the one who is immersed in this condition.

Some Sufis speak about nine stages of love. These are: compatibility, inclination, fellowship, passion, friendship, exclusive friendship, ardent affection, enslavement, and bewilderment.

For most of us, there is more than a little daylight between our spiritual condition as we engage the five pillars and the stage of bewilderment as an expression of the dynamics of love between Creator and created. One might aspire to love God with all one's soul, heart, mind, and strength, but the reality is that most of us fall far short of realizing this aspiration, and the sad fact is that one might not presume that all -- or even a majority of -- Muslims necessarily have such an aspiration.

Seeking to love God is somewhat like making New Year resolutions. It is often done with a sense of sacred commitment that tends to fizzle out in the midst of lived life when we come face to face with just how difficult our own carnal souls make the task to which we have so nobly offered our lives.

Trying to adhere to the five pillars of Islam is a good thing. But trying to accomplish this, and even, if God wishes, succeeding in doing so cannot necessarily be equated with the station of loving God with all one's soul, heart, mind, and strength.

There is a reason why God instructed the Prophet through the Qur'an to tell the bedouins, who claimed they believed, to say, rather, that they submit, because belief had not, yet, entered their hearts. There is a reason why distinctions are drawn among: muslim, mu'min, and mo'hsin, or, islam, iman, and ihsan.

Imam Rauf states:

"By the seventeenth century, two extremely powerful ideas arose in Europe, ideas that paradoxically formed the core of its institutional support for the second commandment [i.e., to love one's neighbor as oneself -- my added note].

-- The notion that reasonable interest on a monetary loan does not amount to usury -- an idea that made possible a certain system of banking.

-- The invention of the corporation, especially that the corporation is a separate 'person' with owners protected from responsibility for any liability, such as unpaid debt or crime, incurred by the company. It is ironic that enormous good has come from the inventions of banking and the corporation ... But these two institutions combined with the emergence of modern liberal democracy to radically improve the fortunes of the Western world. ... Not being able to accept these ideas is one of the primary reasons the Muslim world lagged behind the West and Asian Pacific nations." (Page 3, *What's Right With Islam.*)

Earth calling Commander Tom! Earth Calling Commander Tom! Hello, is anyone there?

One would be hard-pressed to find a more perverse form of argument than to say that at the heart of western institutional support for the second commandment (i.e., loving one's neighbor as one love's oneself) is the invention of interest-based banking and the limited liability corporation. I can't think of anyone -- except perhaps a banker -- who would believe (without blushing with thorough embarrassment) that an act of loving oneself was to charge oneself interest and, therefore, charging interest to one's neighbors is the loving thing to do.

A bank will rarely, if ever, do anything in which there is not something in it for the bank. In fact, a bank will rarely do anything unless things are arranged in such a manner that no matter what happens to anyone else, the bank will come out of things a distinct winner.

This is sort of similar to the case with the 'House' in gambling establishments. The only difference is that banks call on the courts to settle all outstanding debts, rather than seeking the services of people with deformed noses pushed to one side of their faces and who go by names like "Lefty" and "The Animal".

I don't consider this an expression of love. It might be one way of doing business, but it isn't love.

To complicate matters a little, one should not forget compound interest. This is one aspect of things that really gets the saliva of bankers working overtime.

Think of it. Charging interest on interest and not having to do anything for this added bonus except to collect and, when necessary, sue and foreclose.

Of course, one might argue that banks show their love for their neighbors by permitting people to buy, for example, houses and, to make things easy for the customer, arranging for low payments over, say, a 25 year period. When one does the math -- and depending on the interests rates ... whether these are fixed or floating -- by the time someone gets done paying for the house, they have paid anywhere from 4 to 8 times what the market value of the house is worth.

And, let us not forget that one pays most (the vast majority) of the interest up front to the bank before one's payments begin to nibble away at the principle. So, if something should happen somewhere along the line to adversely affect one's capacity to earn an income that is capable of paying the mortgage payment, then even if one has paid interest amounting to more than the value of the house, the bank gets to foreclose, take control of the house and the property on which it is situated, and do the whole thing over again. Now, this is real love! ... Please excuse me for a moment while I wipe a tear from my eye.

We should also remember with fondness and gratitude the Savings and Loans banks who ended up losing billions of dollars and, in the best spirit of sharing, had American taxpayers foot the bill for the irresponsible speculations and business dealings bequeathed to us by these paragons of the commandment to love one's neighbor as oneself.

Moreover, one would be remiss if one were to not make at least a passing reference to all of the most recent 2008-2009 fiascoes involving banks and insurance companies that are 'too big to fail' ... banks and insurance companies and investment houses that just so loved the American people and desired nothing more than to be shown love by those people in the form of multi-billion bailouts. After all, the great unwashed masses are just too stupid to understand how becoming caught up in the derivatives market was all done for the benefit of the public and with such great risk to the banks. And what would the banks get in return for all of their risk-taking on behalf of the people, why nothing but billions of dollars in profits until, of course, margins were called and the bottom fell out and of the derivatives market, and, naturally, it only seems fair that the public should subsidize the losses that accrued as a result of these many manifestations of the bankers love for the community ... I mean, we are all in this together, aren't we?

In addition, let us not forget the World Bank and the International Monetary Fund. These institutions manifest what might be called 'tough love'. As a condition for giving loans, they require countries to restructure society in ways that are bad for most of the inhabitants of that country but that are quite profitable for the leaders, bankers, or foreign corporations within the countries to whom the money is loaned.

Among the requirements that are expected to be instituted by the country receiving such loans are: lower wages, provide no benefits to workers, cut social assistance programs, require poor peasants to pay for health care and education, degrade environmental standards, discourage, if not eliminate (both literally and figuratively) attempts to unionize, tear down the trade barriers that will enable foreign corporations to exploit the resources and people of the country on the cheap, while, simultaneously, destroying local, indigenous economies, and, thereby, force mass migration of peasants to urban areas where they can live in slums and serve as a cheap pool of labor for the government and corporations. Our cups runneth over with the sweet wine of love being poured by the World Bank and the International Monetary Fund.

The people of the countries to whom these loans are given have little, or no, say in what their governments commit those people to. Like the limited liability corporations with which Imam Rauf is so enamored, governments can do almost anything they want with the money that is being loaned, and the common people are the ones who will be on the hook for the debt.

Governments, like many limited liability corporations, love to socialize costs while privatizing profits. The common people subsidize the lifestyle of the government officials by incurring debt that the former did not ask for but that was imposed on them by the thoughtfulness and benevolence of the latter officials who, as we all know, are the protectors and defenders of democracy and all that humankind holds sacred (it is hard to keep a straight face in relation to such a statement).

After government officials siphon off portions of the loan for their own, personal enrichment, and following the distribution of the appropriate bribes and inducements to an assortment of vested interests (such as land owners, rich business people, and other sectors of the country's plutocracy), and after the government spends money on beefing up national security by buying weapons from foreign corporations and paying advisors to teach the national military how to oppress the people of their own country who are likely to get a little testy over the re-structuring process that is about to be foisted on them, then what remains of the loans can be used to help subsidize foreign corporations to further rape the country. So much love is being bestowed on the rank and file people of these countries ... I just don't know how they stand it.

In the United States, 88% of the wealth of the country is owned by just 10 % of the people. Nearly 50% of the wealth of America is owned by 1 % of the people.

Interest charging banks and limited liability corporations (with a considerable helping hand from all three branches of government), have arranged things this way in the United States. The situation is even worse in many other countries.

A number of years ago, I taught a course in criminology for the law and security division of a community college. The textbook I used indicated that, year in and year out, limited liability corporations are responsible for more deaths and theft of money -- and by a substantial margin -- than all forms of street crime combined (including drugs).

I taught the course about thirty years ago. Things have only gotten worse.

All one has to do is mention a few words to help demonstrate the truth of this. For instance, for a starter, try: Enron, Union Carbide, any of the tobacco companies, Exxon, Halliburton, WorldCom, Bank of Credit and Commerce International (BCCI), Monsanto, and Arthur Andersen.

There are hundreds of corporations that could be added to this list. Among other things, these companies specialize in: stealing money from employees, placing employees and the general population in harm's way (either financially and/or environmentally), defrauding the public, and/or being recipients of all manner of corporate welfare handouts that are paid for by taxpayers.

Not every corporation is morally challenged. Many try to be good corporate neighbors, and some even succeed at this -- although, unfortunately, all too frequently this comes with certain costs attached to it in the way of tax concessions from the state and local municipalities or an unwritten agreement for various environmental regulatory laws not to be enforced.

Like Herr Doktor Frankenstein's infamous creation, the limited liability corporation has 143 become something of a monster. This monster, however, unlike Frankenstein's creation, is not fictional ... it is all too real.

Given the natural inclination of human beings toward: greed, arrogance, pride, selfishness, cruelty, and oppression of others, and given this is the case with respect to a species of being who lives, on average, for 70+ years (at least in the United States), and given that human beings are said to have a potential for morality and a sense of justice, if not fairness, and despite this potential, nevertheless, all too many human beings give in to their natural inclinations, and, in so doing, wreak havoc on Earth, then what might we expect when we permit an "artificial person" to be invented that has: perpetual life; unlimited appetites for power, money, and property; an almost complete freedom from any mode of accountability, an absence of morality, and absolutely no sense of shame?

Furthermore, let us add one further ingredient into the laboratory flask. Let us create legal precedents (e.g., Dodge v. Ford, 1916) that make it mandatory for such artificial persons to serve only its prime directive – that is, to maximize returns on investments on 'pain' of legal remedies being applied to chastise any miscreant who does not permit the artificial person from fulfilling its purpose.

Whatever 'good' might have arisen from such an invention, the good has, for the most part, only accrued to the few (remember, 88% of all wealth in the U. S. is owned by only 10% of the people, and these figures are worse in many other countries), and this has come with huge costs being levied against society as a whole. War, degradation of the environment, unsafe working conditions, the exploitation of nonrenewable resources, oppression, the corruption of democratic processes, the corporate biasing of media, loss of worker rights or protections, and the undermining of the judicial process are just a few of the costs that have been borne by the vast majority of people.

Why would the Muslim world want to accept such a creature into its midst? In fact, whenever and wherever such a creature has been accepted into the Muslim world, this has brought -- except for the few -- little but suffering, loss of liberty, oppression, and war.

As a Muslim, I believe one's apportioned allotment is assigned by God. One might have to struggle to realize one's portion, but whatever is destined for one, in the way of material/financial blessings, will come quite independently of interest-charging banks and limited liability corporations.

One of the choices that any human being has is the decision to seek what is destined for one through permissible or impermissible means ... through means that are moral and just, or immoral and unjust. There is something inherently problematic about seeking to serve an entity that has no soul and feels no need to be ashamed before Divinity. There is something deeply disturbing about the idea that the reason why the Muslim world lags behind the West is because of its refusal to bow down before the corporate idol that has been fashioned from gold.

The Qur'an says:

"And surely We shall test you with some fear and hunger and loss of wealth and lives and crops; but give glad tidings to the steadfast - who say when misfortune strikes them: Surely, to Allah we belong and to Allah is our returning." (2:155-156)

The world of corporations and modern banking are two misfortunes that have struck the entire world ... Muslim and non-Muslim alike. The task facing us all in the midst of these misfortunes is to find ways of remaining steadfast with integrity.

There are better ways to distribute justice and material goods to humankind than through the artificial persons known as transnational corporations and banks. Real human beings have the potential for finding far better solutions to the problems besetting humankind than can artificial persons who are, for the most part, little more than sociopaths in many of their behaviors.

One cannot measure or evaluate the economic efficiency of a given process until one adds up all of the costs that are entailed by such a process. Corporations are engaged in a zero-sum game in which they win and everybody else loses -- not necessarily in the surface transactions of such an entity -- but this is so when one looks at all of the hidden costs of permitting corporations to do business as 'artificial people' who enjoy all the privileges and rights of non-artificial people - - and, actually, even more privileges -- but who have no dimension of moral sensibility, public accountability, or commitment to justice for everyone, then one begins to understand that the bottom line for a corporation and the bottom line for society, as a whole, add up in two entirely different ways.

Large corporations -- to the extent that they are 'successful'-- are efficient only when one narrows the focus to issues revolving about ROI (return on investment) and excludes from consideration almost every other dimension of the costly ramifications of the dynamics between corporations and the rest of society. In almost any way one cares to calculate things, the concept of the limited liability corporation has been antithetical to the establishment of real democracy, justice, liberty and the pursuit of happiness for the vast majority of people in any given society in which the idea of corporations as an artificial person has been permitted to take root.

One might come a lot closer to the truth of why the Muslim world has lagged behind the West economically if one takes a closer look at how the military-industrial complex of the West has managed to corrupt -- and, if it cannot corrupt, then to kill, overthrow, control, extort, hold hostage, or remove from office -- virtually every Muslim government for the past several hundred years. So-called Muslim leaders have, by and large, betrayed the generality of Muslims by engaging in illicit intercourse with the 'artificial persons' who have been whispering sweet nothings into the ears and numbered bank accounts of such so-called leaders.

Moreover, all too many imams, mullahs, theologians, Muslim journalists, educators, shaykhs, and qadis (legal judges) have betrayed the vast generality of Muslims by seeking to indoctrinate the latter through methods of spiritual abuse that have, by and large, closed off the populace to what Islam actually is. As a result, many Muslims no better understand the nature of the spiritual abuses that have been perpetrated against them than do the vast majority of Americans understand how limited liability corporations and banks have torn to shreds much of the fabric of democracy in the United States.

Indeed, there has been a massive failure of leadership both among Muslims and Americans that has led to the betrayal of essential principles and values in the United States and in the Muslim world alike. This is one of the experiential truths that Americans and Muslims share.

-----

5) Common Roots

In *What's Right With Islam* Imam Rauf says:

"There is little doubt today that the rise of religious fundamentalism represented the reaction of religion against the antireligious secular modernism that peaked in the mid-twentieth century." (page xx of Preface)

I'm not so sure the foregoing is correct. Essentially, fundamentalism is not an expression of spirituality but, rather, constitutes a desire for power that appears in the guise of a religious form. The power in question has to do with a desire to impose one's perspective on others quite irrespective of the presence of secular modernism ... although secular modernism can assume the role of a stage prop that can be used to incite the emotions of a target audience that fundamentalists seek to control in order to bring about the agenda of the latter.

This tendency to seek power and control over the lives of others existed within the Muslim community from a very early period ... just like it exists, as a potential, within all communities -- both religious and non-religious. Historically, Muslim theologians were often motivated by the desire for such power – that is, a desire to expand their sphere of influence by establishing and imposing the religious norms to which the theologians believed everyone should be subject. Similarly, Muslim jurists frequently were inclined toward such an agenda and, thereby, sought to enforce a certain conception of life upon everyone within the community, and, as well, many Muslim politicians were operating out of a similar sort of framework in which the ultimate goal was to rule over people rather than serve God even as the idea of the latter was used to hide a program of authoritarian control.

Whatever the actual sins of modernism, colonialism, imperialism, and capitalism might be – and these sins are many – the fact of the matter is that those in the Muslim community (theologians, jurists, political rulers) who were either jockeying for power or who were attempting to hold on to power used the very real sins of colonialism et al as a means of misdirecting attention away from their own sins (that is, those of the would-be Muslim "leaders") of wishing to control, exploit, and abuse Muslim peoples. Among fundamentalists, the issue was never – except superficially -- about defending Muslims from the Western hordes but was, rather, an attempt to make sure that the reins of oppression were held by so-called 'Muslims' rather than Westerners.

If one takes a look at the long list of fundamentalists from: the karijis [a sect that came into being during the Caliphacy of Hazrat 'Ali (may Allah be pleased with him) and who – that is, the kharijis – considered all Muslims who did not accept their interpretation of Islam to be infidels], down through: ibn Taymiyyah [1268-1328 who, among other things glorified the idea of jihad – which he construed in terms of armed conflict – to be superior to Islamic pillars such as fasting and the hajj or pilgrimage], Muhammad al-Wahhab [1703 – 1792 who was a founder of a radical, puritanical, dogmatic theology that calls for a return to medieval Islam], Muhammad Abdus Salam Faraj [1952- 1982 who argued that all of the problems existing in the Muslim world were the result of a failure by Muslims to consider jihad -- in the sense of armed, violent conflict -- to be a mandatory duty of every Muslim in relation to combating all non-Muslims as well as those who were 'insufficiently' Muslim], and such groups as the Taliban, al-Qaidah, Hamas, and Hezbollah (along with many other individuals and groups who have not been noted above), all of these groups and individuals have one thing in common – the desire to recreate the world in their own image, using force and compulsion wherever necessary. The common thread among the foregoing fundamentalists is very resonant with the motivation running through modernism, colonialism, imperialism, and capitalism – namely, a desire to impose one's 'will to power' upon innocent people, along with the presumption accompanying this 'will to power' – namely, that one has the right to manipulate and oppress the lives of others.

Rallying cries revolve around this or that cause (whether this be the panicked hysteria in the

West concerning religious fundamentalism, or the frenzied mobs in the East focused on the evils of capitalism and imperialism), but these rallying cries are just techniques of manipulation used by both sides for purposes of creating and managing the fear of various communities. People who are afraid constitute a formidable resource that has been mined for centuries by those who wish to exploit that resource to the advantage of the 'leaders' and to the disadvantage of the people who are sacrificed while fear is stoked to a burning rage all around the world.

To be sure, there are those in the Muslim world who are quite prepared to kill anyone who does not think as the former do. However, there also are people in the West who are quite prepared to kill all who stand in the way of capitalistic or 'democratic' hegemony – whether of an economical, political, and/or militaristic sort. The existence of such real threats is just a pretext that can serve to generate undue influence upon populations – both East and West – in order to induce those respective populations to act out of fear rather than insight, understanding, compassion, or wisdom.

Like actors in a gangster movie, the players on whatever side (West or East) were, and are, interested only in being able to impose their own will on other human beings. The conflict was not and is not a clash of cultures as Huntington tries to argue but, instead, a clash of mobsters and tyrants who were, and are, seeking to slice up the worldly pie in a manner that was, and is, advantageous to any given mobster organization – whether Muslim or non-Muslim.

153

Imam Rauf indicates that being "told that Islam is a religion of peace doesn't jive with images of Muslims" advocating violence against America, Christians, or Jews. On the other hand, being told that the West stands for democracy, freedom, and justice doesn't jive with images of Western corporations, governments, and militaries destroying lives, communities, and countries all over the world while they plunder resources of various peoples that have been usurped by oppressive tyrants in such communities and countries ... tyrants who often are created, funded, supported, armed, trained, and protected by the West.

All too many people in the West and East seem to forget that Jesus (peace be upon him) is reported to have raised a question about those who would find fault with the mote in the eye of one's neighbor while ignoring the beam in one's own eye. Framing the issues becomes very important in the war to control how people think and feel about any given situation. Attention is always directed away from the beam in one's own eye so that one self-righteously can point out the mote in the eye of the other as being the source of the world's problems.

Acting in inhuman ways becomes so much easier when people – with the help of the media, government officials, and religious figures - - can define a problem in terms of the barbaric and uncivilized acts of 'the Other' while completely ignoring the etiological role played by the many atrocities perpetrated against the Other prior to the onset of the Other's treacherous acts – atrocities that are largely or totally ignored by a given side's way of framing things in a self-serving, distorted, and self-righteous manner. The other side is always the causal agent for the existence of evil in the world, when, in truth, events are almost always due to a more complicated dynamic in which forces and factors from all sides converge and synergistically interact with one another to generate crisis, escalation, and tragedy.

Early in *What's Right With Islam* Imam Rauf speaks a little about the First Amendment of the U.S. Constitution, referring to that aspect of the amendment that addresses the issue of the relationship between church and state. He indicates how the founding fathers wished to ensure that religion would not be able to gain access to the corridors of power and, in the process, be imposed upon people. However, Imam Rauf indicates that later on, during the twentieth century, a more militant, anti-religious form of secularism began to hold sway within the institutions of governance, thereby violating what he believed to be the actual intent of the First Amendment authors that, according to Imam Rauf, was never meant to create an atheistic or agnostic society.

Trying to figure out the intent of the founding fathers is a tricky business. Legislatures, courts, jurists, educators, and commentators have been trying to do this for more than two hundred years.

There are, at least, several components to this hermeneutical task. First, there is the intent of the people who actually drafted the amendment, and, secondly, there is the intent of those who voted on the amendment.

Even if there are written records to document, to a degree, what the drafters of an amendment were thinking when a given amendment was proposed, there might not be a great deal of information that details the thinking process of those who voted for or against such an amendment. Did the thinking of the latter coincide precisely with that of the drafters of an amendment, or did it differ, and, if so, in what way? How did they envision the amendment playing out in the actual course of events? What did they believe the constraints and degrees of freedom of such an amendment to be? What did they believe they were signing on to or rejecting?

Were all the people who voted on the amendment inclined toward religion, and, if so, in what way were they religious? Were they orthodox something or other? What did orthodoxy mean to them? Did they have a formal affiliation with religious institutions, or were they independent thinkers and doers when it came to religious observance? What role did they believe government should play in supporting and helping people to seek and, possibly, secure the purpose of life? What did they believe the purpose of life to be?

In order for someone, such as Imam Rauf, to make a statement about what the intention of the founding fathers was, or was not, with respect to the First Amendment, one would have to be able to answer all of the foregoing questions and quite a few more. Imam Rauf might, or might not, be correct in his opinion concerning the intent of the founding fathers, but this is an empirical question that requires evidence not just unsupported supposition.

More importantly, perhaps, there is an issue concerning the First Amendment that Imam Rauf – along with many others – does not seem to consider. If I understand his position, he feels there should be some sort of balance between the aspirations of the state and the aspirations of religion such that while the latter should never be permitted to dominate activities of state, nonetheless, the state should not oppose or undermine the attempts of religious people to give active expression to their individual faith.

One question that I have with respect to the foregoing is this: Why should the state be permitted to have any aspirations at all? Another question I have is the following: Why should the aspirations of the state be permitted to dominate people's lives and be imposed on them if one prevents religion from doing this very same thing?

If the First Amendment is intended, in part, as a safeguard against the unwarranted intrusion of any given religious framework into the lives of the people, then why should one permit the intrusion of any given political framework into the lives of people? If the purpose of this aspect of the First Amendment is to ensure that people do not become unwilling victims of the imposed religious aspirations of others, then, why is there not a reciprocal protection against the imposed political, economic, and philosophical aspirations of others? Why are political and economic philosophies being given a free pass with respect to retaining the right to be imposed on unwilling recipients? If the idea of this facet of the First Amendment is to protect the people against being oppressed by a religion not of their own choosing, then why are the people not being protected against being oppressed by political philosophies, economic programs, and public policies not of their own choosing? Why is the presumption of governance being given to philosophy – whether this is political, economic, and/or social in nature?

Oppression is oppression whether it comes from religion or politics. If the majority were of a given religious denomination, we do not say: 'Well, the will of the majority should be enforced but, rather, one points to the First Amendment and indicates that no religion – irrespective of its majority status – might dominate state policy'.

In a sense, this portion of the First Amendment is directed toward protecting the rights of minorities against the imposition of religious beliefs. No such protections are afforded minorities against the imposition of unwanted political and philosophical beliefs.

I find this to be a curious asymmetry. Is one to suppose that politics and philosophy are somehow more objective or more neutral or less biased than religion is? Is one to assume that politics and philosophy are inherently more humane, just, and compassionate than any religion could be? Is one to automatically presume that politics and philosophy are better equipped to be less arbitrary, oppressive and authoritarian than religions are?

What and where is the evidence to support such presumption? Why is it okay to rule over people in the name of politics, economics, or philosophy, but not okay to rule over people in the name of religion?

Irrespective of what the founding fathers might, or might not, have thought about such matters, I agree with the idea that religion ought not to become entangled in the principles of governance in such a way that religion is imposed on the community being governed. At the same time, I also believe that politics, economics, and philosophy ought not to become entangled in the principles of governance in such a way that they are imposed on the community being governed.

If one agrees that the principles inherent in protecting people from having religion imposed on them are valuable safeguards against tyranny and oppression, then consistency requires that the same principles be applied to safeguard the public against the tyranny and oppression inherent in any political, philosophical, or economic system that is imposed on others without their consent. Moreover, if people do not wish to be consistent in the manner in which they seek to protect the community against tyranny and oppression, then one needs to inquire into the nature of the motivation underlying this inconsistency and preferential asymmetry.

Imam Rauf claims that:

"Muslims believe that America needs to reestablish the original understanding of the First Amendment, that balances the separation of church and state with freedom of religion by allowing all religions equal standing and by honoring the role of religion in building a good society. This balance is enormously important to Muslims."

Aside from the fact that I find it somewhat disconcerting to be told that Muslims believe 'such and such' when I am a Muslim, and I don't necessarily believe what Imam Rauf says I believe, and aside from the already mentioned idea that I'm not sure that what he claims the original intention or understanding of the First Amendment to be actually constitutes the original understanding of all parties who voted on that amendment, I also wonder about the meaning of the idea of 'balance' to which he alludes in his foregoing claim.

How does one maintain a separation of church and state in a balanced way? What are the criteria by which one evaluates the conditions of balance? What methodologies are to be used in analyzing the idea of balance? What assumptions underlie such criteria and methodologies? How does one define the "good society"? What justifies such a definition?

For example, suppose a person's spiritual perspective holds that killing is wrong, as well as maintains that most wars are not about protecting the homeland but advancing the special interests of various corporations, power blocs, and ideological agendas, then 'collateral damage' is really a euphemism for cold-blooded murder and not just an 'unfortunate' side effect of that which is necessary (and necessity here is always framed by those who are seeking to advance their economic, political, material, and/or financial interests). How does one 'balance' such a perspective with the perspective of those who have no problem with taking innocent human lives if this will further their worldly goals? Why should the former be required to support (e.g., through taxes) the perpetration of that (i.e., murder and oppression) to which they do not subscribe, and why should they have to be subjected to the possibility of being charged with 'treasonous' behavior simply because they do not want to lend the kind of support that violates their sense of right and wrong?

There is no balance here. An almost automatic preference tends to be given to the war-mongers, as well as to those with vested material/financial interests and to those who have an ideological agenda that they wish to oppressively impose on people, both domestic and foreign, and the question is why are there no protections against such political, philosophical, and economic tyranny if a central purpose of the 1st amendment is to ensure that oppressive elements do not control governance and if one of the central purposes of the Bill of Rights is to protect, among other things, disempowered minorities against the tyranny of majority rule?

Religion is about meaning, purpose, identity, values, and potential. Philosophy and politics are about meaning, purpose, identity, values, and potential. How does one balance conflicting and sometimes diametrically opposed ways of setting about to answer questions concerning such themes?

If the founding fathers believed in such a balance, then what, precisely, did they mean by this? Did they really understand what they were advocating or voting on? Did they have it all worked out, or was it something of a rough idea whose structural character and horizons were lost in shadows of unasked questions and unknown contingencies?

If one were to bring the founding fathers together today and ask them about whether they truly believed in the idea of allowing all religions equal standing and whether, or not, the founding fathers wanted to honor the role of all religion in building a good society, how would they respond? Would they maintain that, for example, Islam, Hinduism, Buddhism, Taoism, as well as the spiritual ways of various Native peoples constituted authentic religious traditions and ought to be accorded equal standing and honored for the way in which they contributed to the building of a good society? And, if they truly believed all these things, then why – to raise but one issue -- were Native peoples treated in such abysmal, destructive, inhumane ways from the very beginning?

Imam Rauf goes on to say that:

"Muslims have yet to fully incorporate the institutional expressions of democratic capitalism ... into their various essential institutions: the rule of law (an independent judiciary), human rights, a stable currency, equal opportunity, free markets, social safety nets, and so forth. These principles, in my view, are among the most important institutional expressions of the second commandment that humanity has invented."

Notwithstanding the problems I might have with Imam Rauf's tendency, from time to time, to make sweeping generalizations about what Muslims have, or have not, done across all geographical areas and historical periods, and aside from any questions that I might have about what it would mean to "fully incorporate" such institutional expressions of democratic capitalism or whether even the West has yet to accomplish this, I have a lot of difficulty with the mythology being spewed forth with respect to the alleged accomplishments of 'democratic capitalism'.

For instance, one could talk about the manner in which the judiciary has often been anything but independent as they (across all levels – from municipal, to county, state, and federal) frequently served the interests of power, capital and corporations against the interests of the poor and unempowered. As far as human rights are concerned, one might want to speak with Native peoples, Blacks, women and other minority groups who subsist along the margins of enjoying the full protections of human rights. Moreover, we don't have a stable currency, we have a floating value currency that has been set loose from any meaningful backing by actual material value (e.g., gold or silver), and the jury is still out as to how long the whole financial house of cards will survive before it falls apart, as has occurred on so many occasions throughout U.S. history. In the matter of 'equal opportunity', there are tens of millions of people in the United States who do not have equal opportunity with respect to education, jobs, housing, legal representation, medical care, or government access. In addition, the markets are not free but are distorted by such forces as: government subsidies, corporate welfare, a judiciary that lacks sufficient intelligence to understand that a corporation is not a person, an inequitable system of taxation, regulatory agencies that dance to the beat of lobbyists, and corrupt politicians who serve vested interests against the interests of the people they supposedly represent and against the interests of a truly free system of enterprise. Finally, it is difficult to get excited about a social safety net that has so many rips and tears that millions upon millions of people have fallen through the holes in that safety net.

Imam Rauf maintains that what America has done right is to create institutions that have perfected democratic capitalism. At any moment I expect Rod Serling to step out of the shadows and begin to talk about a man (namely Imam Rauf) who does not yet seem to understand that he has become trapped in the Twilight Zone as this inhabitant of a surreal realm addresses people as if his perceptions and beliefs defined the true nature of things even though what is being discussed by Imam Rauf is not perfected, is not really democratic, and constitutes a perverted, re-framed notion of what capitalism might have been if it had been guided by qualities of justice, morality, and spirituality rather than qualities of greed, inhumanity, and oppression.

Early in Chapter 1 of *What's Right With Islam*, Imam Rauf outlines how many of the earliest civilizations advocated acceptance of, or belief in, a variety of gods with each god being assigned a particular section of the universe over which to exercise authority. He goes on to indicate that the leaders of such civilizations – whether called a king, pharaoh, emperor, Caesar, czar, or potentate – were often considered god-like and that the rest of the population were born into one class or another -- ranging from: priestly, to: warrior, noblemen, farmer, merchant, financier, and the like – who performed roles within the greater society that allegedly served the greater good of a divinity, empire, and/or ruler.

Those who did not wish to accept the way things were set up and worked tended to be considered as traitors. Such individuals were usually ostracized, jailed, executed, or some combination of the three.

In many ways, things really haven't changed all that much. Corporations, nations, and so-called 'leaders' work out arrangements – either violently or peacefully – to divvy up the known universe into fiefdoms over which they exercise control. Now they go by the title of president, premier, prime minister, governor, or CEO.

These individuals often consider themselves to be god-like and frequently are treated as gods by their groupies, supporters, and underlings. The task of these leaders is to induce everyone else to serve what is referred to as the greater good, and almost invariably the 'greater good' is equivalent to whatever agenda the leaders are pushing at any given time ... an agenda that serves the needs of the 'leaders' and not necessarily the needs of the millions of people who, often unwittingly, assist the leaders to realize their agenda..

Nowadays, class is not necessarily a function of inherited roles such as farmer, merchant, religious cleric, warrior, and so on – although things sometimes do work out this way. Today, class is a function of money along with the power that accompanies such money, and, for the most part, people who begin wealthy stay wealthy, and those who begin poor remain poor.

The classes are fairly rigid in this sense with a limited number of exceptions to the general rule used to shore up the untenable argument that anyone can succeed in today's world. Yes, there are an abundance of rags to riches stories that are trotted out for purposes of propaganda, but, the reality of the matter is that there is only a very limited amount of vertical financial movement that is possible in today's world, and there is even less vertical movement when it comes to acquiring any meaningful sort of power within the structure of modern societies.

Moreover, as was true in the times of earlier civilizations, so too, today, those who are not in accord with the modern way of divvying up power, resources, and money are branded as traitors and, as a result, are ostracized, punished, jailed, executed, or some combination of the four. Some people like to think that substantial progress has been made when one compares early civilizations and present society, but, in all too many ways, nothing really has changed except names, dates, and titles.

According to Imam Rauf we are all free to think for ourselves and that the very idea of mind control is an anathema to any society that purports to be free. Even if one were to agree with Imam Rauf that we might be free to think for ourselves, individuals in this society are often not free to act on what they think (without facing severe sanctions such as loss of a job and/or career, financial hardship, ridicule by the media, or becoming a community outcast), and if one is not free within the sphere of activity, then one has to question the value of merely being able to think in a free manner that has little, or no, spillover into the realm of action.

However, putting aside for the moment the relationship between thinking and activity – which is a very complex, multifaceted problem within a pluralistic society – one might question how many people in this society are really free to even <u>think</u> for themselves. When one learns that five years after September 11, 2001, more than 40% of the people who listen to Fox News still believe there is a connection between Saddam Hussein and the tragedies of 9/11 and/or that Saddam Hussein and al-Qaida were co-conspirators in the events of 9/11 ... something that even President Bush finally admitted was not the case -- after much hemming, hawing, and many misleading statements by both him and Vice President Cheney on the matter -- then, really, how much of this 40% of the Fox listening audience can be thinking for themselves? When we live in an age when groups like 'the Swift-boat Veterans For Truth' or all too many talk radio hosts, along with media outlets that are financially dependent on corporate owners, sponsors, and advertisers, can, and do, muddy the waters with the express purpose of re-framing events in a distorted manner and, as a result, many recipients of these propaganda campaigns begin to treat distortion and bias as if they were fact ... when we exist within a environment of intentionally nurtured fear concerning non-existent entities such as 'weapons of mass destruction' that are used as a pretext for raining down upon other societies our actual weapons of mass destruction ... when we live at a time when we are not only urged, but expected to (with a potential for being penalized if we do not) accept the findings of a 9/11 Commission that did not have the time, money, security clearance, subpoena power, will, mandate, or integrity to actually get at the truth of 9/11 and was politically compromised from the very beginning by the very vested interests who were inherently opposed to a truly free and rigorous examination of an 'official story' that does not stand up to even casual critical examination ... when we grow up within a compulsory educational environment in which both American and world history are often air-brushed by teachers and textbooks with the cosmetics of mythology, rationalization, and self-serving biases ... then, really, how free are people to think for themselves?

There are many degrees of freedom through which to think about misinformation, disinformation, bias, error, falsehood, distortion, and delusion. However, if one does not understand that what one is thinking about is untrue, then all the freedom in the world is not necessarily going to help one in any constructive manner.

As Henry Ford is once reported to have said: "You can have any color of car you like as long as it's black." Similarly, all too many people would offer us the idea that we are free to think whatever we like as long as it conforms to the color of belief with which we are provided by those in politics, government, the media, the corporate world, and education who wish to control what we think about and the way in which we think about it.

Imam Rauf refers to the set of values – namely, liberty, equality, social justice, and fraternity ... which he believes to be at the core of monotheistic spiritual traditions such as Judaism, Christianity, and Islam – as the Abrahamic ethic. While in the light of current hostilities among Jews, Christians, and Muslims, it is understandable that Imam Rauf would wish to try to create a basis of common currency among the aforementioned monotheistic traditions by subsuming the above-noted set of values under the rubric of the Abrahamic ethic (millati ibrahim), I also think that this way of doing things carries dimensions of distortion and exclusion with it.

More specifically, the qualities of liberty, equality, social justice and fraternity were part of the message transmitted to humankind by all Prophets, starting with Adam (peace be upon him). The ethic to which this set of qualities gives expression, therefore, did not start with Abraham (peace be upon him) and, consequently, it is not an ethic that he invented or that started with him, but rather, this ethic consisted of principles dealing with morality and conduct that had been given by Divinity to human beings since the time that the latter first started to walk on the face of the Earth.

The fact of the matter is that until Abraham (peace be upon him) received guidance from God, Abraham (peace be upon him) did not know what the truth of things was. As pointed out in the Qur'an, 6: 75-91, he had to go on a spiritual journey, and at one time or another during this quest he questioned whether the moon, stars, or the sun were appropriate objects of worship.

Because God guided Abraham (peace be upon him), the latter was able to navigate through the uncertainties entailed by his consideration of different objects as possible foci for his worship. Without this guidance, Abraham (peace be upon him) would have wandered into the same kinds of errors as did his father and the surrounding community.

Prophets and peoples were guided in this way before Abraham (peace be upon him). The guidance concerned not only the relationship between humankind and Divinity, but the guidance covered, as well, matters involving the relationship of human beings one with another, and, thus, the core set of values encompassing liberty, equality, social justice, and fraternity existed long before the Prophetic mission of Abraham (peace be upon him).

Indeed, as the Qur'an indicates to Muhammad (peace be upon him):

"Verily, We have sent messengers before thee. Among them are some of whom We have told thee, and some of whom we did not tell thee. (40: 78)"

This was as true for Abraham (peace be upon him) as it was for Muhammad (peace be upon him) – there were communities that existed prior to both Abraham and Muhammad (peace be upon them both) that had been sent prophets, books of guidance, and spiritual assistance.

For example, Buddha is not mentioned in the Qur'an, nor is Krishna, nor are the great spiritual personalities of different indigenous peoples. However, perhaps these individuals were, nonetheless, sent by Divinity with guidance –

guidance that included principles covering issues of liberty, equality, social justice and fraternity.

In fact, the so-called founding fathers borrowed a great many of 'their' ideas from the principles by which many Native peoples lived their lives. Representatives from the Native peoples were invited to, attended, and contributed a great many substantial and constructive ideas to a number of pre-Constitutional sessions called by the 'founding fathers'.

These contributions revolved around issues of liberty, equality, social justice, and fraternity. Many of these ideas were incorporated into the framework of the Constitution and, later, the Bill of Rights.

The Qur'an does make reference to the millati (ethic, way, principles, method) of Abraham in, for example, the verse:

"Who forsakes the millati of Abraham except the one who depreciates himself." (2: 130)

Nonetheless, by and large, this millati is consistent with, and reflects, the essence of, the millati that had been taught to people via prophets who came before Abraham (peace be upon him). The millati of Abraham was taught to him just as it was taught to some of those who preceded him, and, so, in reality, the millati Abraham is really the millati of God.

Imam Rauf says:

"While it's true that India, China, and Japan are not generally monotheistic societies, increasingly they are implementing democratic systems of government – systems anchored in the concept of human equality and thus emanating from the Abrahamic ethic. This is the ethic that is embedded in human nature. (page 15)"

However, if what Imam Rauf claims – namely, that the ethic in question is embedded in human nature – is true, then movements toward liberty, equality, and social justice did not emanate from the Abrahamic ethic, but, rather, arose through the presence of Divine guidance in people's lives across time and geographical locales around the world quite independently of Prophet Abraham (peace be upon him).

There have been a lot of different spiritual traditions in India, China and Japan, and one wonders if Imam Rauf is not guilty of a certain amount of overgeneralization, if not distortion, when he claims that these are not generally monotheistic societies. First, one has the problem of trying to disentangle the original nature of a given spiritual tradition from the purely human theological hermeneutics that might have been layered over the original like a complex palimpsest. In other words, even if one were to agree that in some instances there was an absence of what we might recognize as monotheism in the spiritual traditions of such countries, nonetheless, this might be irrelevant to teachings concerning the Oneness of Being that might originally have been taught to human beings through Divine emissaries who had been sent to such societies ... emissaries who are not necessarily mentioned in the Qur'an or the Bible but who are known, nonetheless, to Divinity.

In addition, one could put forth defensible positions that there are strains of Buddhism, Taoism, and the Vedanta – to name just three -- which are rigorously oriented to the idea that Reality is One ... even if terms such as God, Divinity, and theism are not used. These same traditions taught values involving freedom, equality, social justice, and fraternity – values that would resonate with what Imam Rauf considers to be the inherent nature of human beings in general and, therefore, are not necessarily derivative from – although quite consonant with -- what he refers to as the Abrahamic ethic.

Later on (page 33) in his book, Imam Rauf says that:

"Muslims thereby relate to humanity on three levels: to all humanity as humans, to all religious communities as common heirs of a divinely revealed religious tradition, and to Jews and Christians as direct recipients of the Abrahamic ethic as such."

Aside from a failure of the foregoing statement to make a distinction between what Islam calls Muslims to do and what Muslims might actually do [and, unfortunately, not all Muslims do relate to other human beings as fellow members of humankind], in addition, contrary to what Imam Rauf claims not all Muslims relate "to all religious communities as common heirs to a divinely revealed religious tradition". In fact just a small number of pages prior (page 15) to the present quote (page 33), Imam Rauf made comments about how India, China, and Japan are not generally monotheistic societies, and, then indicated on page 32 that the Abrahamic ethic was rooted in a radical monotheism expressed in loving one God with all one's being. So, readers, quite understandably, might have a tendency to become somewhat confused about what Imam Rauf is really saying in this respect.

On page 34 of *What's Right With Islam*, under a section labeled: 'Hindus and Buddhists: Older Kids On The Block', Imam Rauf does cite the Quranic verses (4: 163-164) which stipulate that God has sent many messengers to humankind but Divinity has not disclosed the identities of those messengers to everyone. Based on these verses and a few other citations, Imam Rauf argues that:

"Hindus and Buddhists are descendants from religious teachings originally brought forth from prophets descended from Adam and Noah. (page 35)".

There is a Hadith in which the Prophet Muhammad (peace be upon him) is reported to have said that:

"There are 71 sects among Jews, and only one of them is correct. There are 73 sects among Christians, and only one of them is correct. There are 73 sects among Muslims, and only one of them is correct."

By interpolation, or extrapolation, one might argue that if Hinduism and Buddhism are derived from spiritual "teachings originally brought forth from prophets descended from Adam and Noah", then there are x-number of sects in Hinduism and Buddhism, and, perhaps, only one each is respectively correct.

Based on my reading, studies, and discussions with various Hindus and Buddhists, I believe there is a great deal of truth and wisdom inherent in the Hindu and Buddhist spiritual traditions. Nonetheless, I do not believe that by acknowledging this truth, one is, therefore, compelled to accept every iota of Hindu and Buddhist theology as necessarily being accurately reflective of the original spiritual teachings that were given to prophets in those societies anymore than one should feel obligated to accept every scrap of Muslim, Christian, or Jewish theology that exists as being necessarily accurately reflective of the actual spiritual teachings that were given to prophets in the latter societies.

So, while I am quite willing to recognize – as a general principle – that there are various elements, themes, and teachings within Hinduism and Buddhism that do arise out of, and deeply resonate with, original spiritual teachings that pre-dated the appearance of Hinduism and Buddhism, I am not really sure what Imam Rauf has in mind here because he spends almost no time delineating either of these latter two spiritual traditions. Perhaps, wishing to be something of a diplomat or politician, he is trying to be inclusive without really saying anything at all that might entail hermeneutical difficulties for his position.

However, several recurrent themes in Imam Rauf's book are the Oneness of God and the importance of monotheism to the Abrahamic ethic. Given that there are prominent strains of Hinduism that are inclined to polytheism, and there are prominent strains of Buddhism that are oriented around a non-theistic approach to spirituality, one is not quite sure what Imam Rauf is saying.

Is he playing to the majoritarian reading audience of Christians, Jews, and Muslims, with a few amorphous and ambiguous protective bon mots mentioned in passing with respect to several other religious traditions in order to create, at the very least, an appearance of inclusiveness and acceptance of other spiritual paths? Or, is he being somewhat disingenuous about how he words things? Or, is Imam Rauf just muddled in his thinking on these issues?

Furthermore, I find it interesting that there is no mention of traditions like Taoism or the spirituality of various indigenous peoples such as North American Native peoples, the Aborigines of Australia, or the Maori of New Zealand. To be sure, one cannot explore and discuss everything within a book of limited pages and many purposes, but when a reader is grappling with trying to understand what, precisely, Imam Rauf is saying or arguing, then a few more points of reference in this context than were supplied by him in his book might greatly facilitate matters.

To claim on behalf of Muslims that everyone of us accepts "all religious communities as common heirs to a divinely revealed religious tradition" is just not tenable empirically since there are many Muslims whom I know, or whom I have read about, who would not agree to what Imam Rauf stipulates as being the case in this respect. Moreover, such a claim is not tenable rationally since no one – whether they be Jewish, Christian, Muslim, Hind, Buddhist, Taoist, or from an indigenous spiritual tradition -- could reasonably expect anyone to accept anything and everything that bears the moniker of "religious".

Truth is what it is. Various religious traditions are attempts, some of which are much better than others, to merge horizons with at least certain aspects of that truth, and there are few, if any, who would maintain that any tradition that refers to itself as religious or spiritual necessarily succeeds, wholly or partially, in such efforts.

On page 16 of *What's Right With Islam*, Imam Rauf cites the following Quranic verse – namely:

"Be religious in accordance with your truest inclinations, the immutable nature (fitra) of God upon which He created people – there is no altering God's creation – that is right religiousness, but most people do not know. (30:30)"

Imam Rauf claims:

"That any person who listens to his or her heart or conscience would recognize that God is One, that humanity is one family, that humans should be free and should treat each other fairly and with justice."

Given, as I am quite sure that Imam Rauf would agree, that human beings are inclined to error without the support of Divine guidance and assistance, one might not be able to accept what he says in the foregoing without a certain amount of qualification. One of the lessons of history is that, for the most part, human beings all too frequently are not spiritually in accord with their truest inclinations or fitra since they do not recognize that God is One or that humanity constitutes one family or that human beings ought to be free and ought to treat one another with equitability.

Because the foregoing is very often the nature of human affairs, this is precisely why guidance is necessary and why Divine books and messengers are sent to humankind. If human beings could act in accordance with our truest inclinations or fitra on our own, then Divine guidance would not be necessary, but such does not appear to be the case.

Many people listen to what they believe is their heart or their conscience only to later discover – if they are fortunate -- that the real teachings of the heart, conscience, and fitra are something other than what they previously believed or thought. Not only is the art of listening to one's heart or being in accordance with one's fitra difficult to accomplish, but learning how to differentiate among the different forces – both destructive and constructive – which seek to undermine the proper functioning of the heart, conscience, or fitra -- entails an extremely difficult set of tasks.

In general terms we might all agree that qualities such as freedom, equality, social justice and fraternity are very important. However, both Divinity and the Devil are in the details of working out what any of these qualities actually mean amidst the many particularized problems and complexities of everyday existence.

Like the *Peanuts* character, Linus once said – "I love humanity! It's people I can't stand." Consequently, when one looks into one's heart and conscience, we might all see a tain constructed from general ideas (like Linus's humanity) concerning freedom, equality, social justice, and fraternity, but the <u>particular</u> images of freedom, equality, and so on that are reflected from the glass covering the tain (like Linus's actual people) might be very different from one individual to the next.

For example, I agree with Imam Rauf about the importance of each of the qualities that he mentions. Yet, nonetheless -- as I am pointing out in the present discussion, as well as other essays appearing elsewhere in this collection that critically engage *What's Right With Islam* -- my understanding of these qualities (along with a number of additional themes) seems to be quite different than his conception of what freedom, equality, social justice and fraternity might involve. Some of these differences are minor, but others appear to be much more substantial.

What does it mean to say: that God is One (e.g., there has been an on-going historical controversy between those who maintained that there is a 'oneness of witnessing' but rejected the position of those who advocated a 'oneness of Being', and vice versa), or that humanity is one family (is it a dysfunctional family, or a family beset by internecine struggles like Cain and Abel, or a family locked in unending machinations and manipulations like the brothers of Joseph – peace be upon him)? What degrees of freedom should be extended to any given individual and what degrees of constraint? What do we mean when we say that one should treat others fairly and with justice?

Imam Rauf seeks to draw a parallel between the "self-evident Truths" of the Declaration of Independence and the natural inclination of our minds and heart to acknowledge the truth of the Abrahamic ethic. Yet, initially, these truths of the framers of the Declaration of Independence that were allegedly so self-evident excluded women (unless they were property owners), blacks, slaves, the homeless, and Native peoples from having a rightful place among the men who were "created equal and endowed by their Creator with certain inalienable rights."

Apparently, like the central characters of Orwell's *Animal Farm*: 'All of us are equal, but some of us are more equal than others'. In any event, once again, the idea that all we have to do is look within our conscience and hearts to see the truth of things raises a lot of unanswered questions for a perspective like that which Iman Rauf is putting forth concerning the alleged self-evident nature of the truths about freedom, liberty, social justice, and fraternity.

Is Imam Rauf correct about things, or am I correct about things, or are both of us wrong, or are we partially right and partially wrong? God knows best, but what I do know is that the problem is not as simple as Imam Rauf seems to indicate – that is, we do not just look into our hearts or conscience and realize the nature of fitra. This requires considerable: spiritual guidance, Divine assistance, as well as struggle from ourselves. Indeed, if things were as Imam Rauf appears to suppose them to be, there would be no need for revelation, Prophets, or other forms of Divine assistance.

According to Imam Rauf "those that practice what their hearts tell them are practicing the right religion". The Qur'an refers to this as "deen Allah" (Qur'an, 3: 83), and Imam Rauf says that this 'deen' has been bequeathed to human faculties of reason and understanding. Moreover, Imam Rauf claims, on the one hand, that the primary component of this understanding is the recognition that God is One and, on the other hand, that both jinn and human beings have been created for no other purpose than to worship God – Who "desires no aid from" humans nor jinn (Qur'an 51: 57) – and that the nature of worship "involves the observance of His patterns which are knowable by reason (page 16)".

In the Qur'an one finds the following:

"The seven heavens and the earth and all that is therein praise God and there is nothing that does not glorify God in praise, but you understand not their manner of praise." (17: 44)

Apparently, reason is not enough since we all have it and, yet, there are patterns of praise and worship inherent in the nature of things – including humankind -- which we do not understand.

Abraham's father, who constructed and fashioned idols that gave expression to polytheism rather than monotheism, had reason, but he did not observe or understand or grasp the Divine patterns ... or, perhaps, he did observe such patterns but just interpreted them incorrectly. Might one suppose that Abraham's father looked into his heart or conscience and that reason told him that polytheism was the right way to go? Do we have any evidence to indicate that this was not the case?

Presumably, just looking into one's heart or conscience and working toward a reasoned understanding is not enough. Not all reasoning is necessarily correct. Not everything that we believe our hearts and conscience are telling us is necessarily an accurate reflection of what God might be trying to disclose to us through the signs and patterns of nature, revelation, or prophetic missions. Something is missing from the equation.

In the Qur'an are the following two verses:

"And whoever is blind in this world will be blind in the Hereafter, and even further from the path." (17: 72)

And,

"It is not their eyes which are blind, but the hearts in their breast." (22: 46)

Obviously, according to the Qur'an there are forces that can obscure the vision of the heart. If the vision of the heart is not clear, then various kinds of blindness plague human understanding and reason.

Spiritually speaking, the heart is a capacity with different dimensions, potentials and characteristics. One facet of the heart is known as the 'qalb' – an Arabic term meaning that which turns or fluctuates.

The qalb can be oriented toward the carnal soul, Iblis, and/or the multiplicity of emotional and rationalistic entanglements knows as 'dunya' or the 'world'. The qalb also can be oriented toward the ruh or spirit.

In fact, the qalb is a battleground of forces for both good and evil that determines one's degree of receptivity to spiritually destructive and constructive currents running through the heart. If one is attuned to spiritually destructive currents, then one will be beset with one kind or another of blindness with respect to correct understanding or reasoning. If, on the other hand, one is, by the Grace of God, receptive to spiritually constructive influences running through the heart, then one's understanding and reasoning are modulated in a way that assists one to 'see' and understand some element of truth and to be able to use this understanding to direct reasoning in an efficacious manner.

All of the foregoing can be summed up in a saying that has been attributed to the Prophet Muhammad (peace be upon him).

"There is an organ within the human being which, if it is problematic, then, the whole of one's being becomes problematic, but, if that organ is sound, then, the whole of being is sound, and that organ is the heart."

A little later on in Chapter 1 of *What's Right With Islam* Imam Rauf does indicate that there is a strong tendency within human nature to resist the primordial, spiritual capacity of fitra that God has bestowed upon humankind. He describes this inclination toward resistance as a form of 'forgetfulness' and indicates that this is not primarily a matter of forgetting what we know – that is, a lapse in memory – but, rather, constitutes a failure to apply what we know. In effect, we know better than we often do.

I tend to disagree somewhat with Imam Rauf in relation to the forgoing position. While I do accept the idea that human beings might not act in a way that is consistent with what we know to be right or moral, one has to address the issue of why such inconsistency between knowledge and action arises in the first place. I believe this inconsistency points toward a deeper problem.

Essentially, the problem of forgetting revolves around the issue of identity. We have forgotten who we are. We have forgotten our spiritual potential. We have forgotten our origins. We have forgotten why we have been brought into this world. We have forgotten our relationship with God. We have forgotten how to reconnect with that which we have forgotten.

Even when, by the Grace of God, we recognize something to be true and correct, we often do not act in consort with that understanding because we have forgotten that nothing is possible without Divine support and assistance. We have forgotten that – in the reported words of the Prophet:

"This life is but a tillage for the next life, therefore, do good deeds here that you might reap benefits there … for striving is an ordinance of God, and whatever God has ordained can be attained only by striving."

In short, we have forgotten that effort and struggle is necessary to, among other things, acquire understanding and, then in addition, convert such understanding into appropriate action.

In pre-eternity the Qur'an indicates that Allah addressed the spirits with:

"Am I not your Lord? (Alastu bi rabbikum) And the spirits answered: "'Yes, we testify (Qarbala)'. " (7: 172).

When we were brought into this world, most of us forgot this conversation and the myriad ramifications of the central question and answer of that dialogue.

Furthermore, this inclination toward forgetfulness is not merely a passive phenomenon but can become a very rigorous tendency toward rebelling against anything that might lead to remembering our essential identity and its concomitant responsibilities. More specifically, not only do we have a carnal soul that incites us to forgetfulness, but, as the Qur'an indicates:

"If anyone forsakes the remembrance of the Most Gracious, We appoint a devil to be an intimate companion for that person and who will hinder that individual from the path. Yet, they think they are being guided in the right direction." (43: 36-37)

Therefore, the problem of forgetfulness goes beyond not acting in accordance with what we might know to be right, just, or moral. In fact, this latter kind of forgetfulness can be subsumed under the more essential form of forgetting outlined above – a more essential form of forgetfulness that explains why, among other things, a disparity between knowledge and action arises in the first place.

Imam Rauf goes on to state that:

"If there is anything in the Islamic view that approximates the Christian idea of original sin, in the sense of something that can be described as the universal human flaw, it is that humans forget." (page 23).

I believe this statement to be problematic in several ways.

First of all, the theological concept of original sin usually does not refer to some universal flaw in human beings but rather refers to what is inherited by every human being due to the mistakes of Adam (peace be upon him) and Eve (may Allah be pleased with her) when they disobeyed God in the Garden of Eden. This is the sin for which people are said – at least by many Christians – to be in need of baptism ... for which even Jesus (peace be upon him) was supposedly required to be baptized by John the Baptist (peace be upon him) ... although there are aspects of baptism, depending on which brand of Christian theology one is considering, that extend beyond just the need to be cleansed of original sin and that enter into a condition of complete spiritual renewal.

To speak in terms of a potential for rebellion against the truth (i.e., the nafs or carnal soul) is a very different idea than is the notion of original sin. Although, spiritually speaking, all human beings do inherit the capacity to rebel against truth, this capacity has to be acted upon through choice – that is, one has to choose to rebel in order for this aspect of human potential to be given expression. However, in the matter of original sin, one gets no choice in the matter – one inherits the stain of sin without ever exercising choice. This is diametrically opposed to the Islamic perspective in which all human beings are born innocent and sin-free and, then the intentions and choices of life determine whether, or not, we commit spiritual errors for which we are to be held accountable.

Imam Rauf develops a general framework for some of the problems that arose following the passing away of the Prophet Muhammad (peace be upon him) from this world. These included: the generating of written manuscripts that were faithful to the recited Qur'an; the emergence of practice of tafsir that was an exegetical practice that focused on delineating the circumstances surrounding the occurrence of any given instance of revelation in an attempt to gain insight into the meaning of such revelation relative to the nature of the historical and social context in which such revelations emerged; and, the development of fiqh, or theories of jurisprudence, as ways of organizing and regulating society.

The foregoing problems are presented against the backdrop of a challenge that Imam Rauf believes faces every faith tradition – namely, how to translate original teachings into a form that not only makes sense to a different set of historical and sociological circumstances but, as well, preserves the essential truths of the original teachings. Moreover, he points out that, generally speaking, the tendency down through history has been for divisions to arise within the community out of which a given expression of Divine guidance arose.

For instance, he mentions the rift that took place following the termination of the initial Earthly mission of Jesus (peace be upon him) between the Jewish and Christian communities even though Jesus is reported to have said that he does 'not come to reject what came before (i.e., Judaism) but to confirm it and add to it.' And, Imam Rauf also alludes to divisions within the Muslim community about issues of propriety surrounding the creation of a written Qur'an, the nature of tafsir, and the rise of various schools of religious jurisprudence in relation to Islam.

Imam Rauf proceeds to cite a verse of the Qur'an that he feels reflects on the foregoing situation of divisiveness:

"[God] ordained for you of religion that which He enjoined upon Noah, and We have revealed to you, and that We enjoined on Abraham and Moses and Jesus – to establish religion (deen) and to not be divided therein." (42: 13)

Imam Rauf then summarizes what he believes to be one of the teachings of the foregoing verse – namely, that "divisive attitudes and practices are signs of a non- or anti-monotheistic, anti-Abrahamic ethic." (page 29)

To state what would appear to be an obvious point, if all we have to do is look into our hearts and conscience in order to grasp the truth of the Abrahamic ethic as Imam Rauf earlier argued, then how is the kind of divisiveness noted above possible? Even when there is agreement that it is the deen (or spiritual method and way) of Noah, Abraham, Moses, Jesus, and Muhammad (peace be upon them all) which should be followed, differences emerge with respect to establishing the precise nature of that deen.

Moreover, prophets were consistently charged with introducing divisiveness into their respective communities by those who were opposed to them. So, how does one differentiate the establishing of truth -- which always encroaches on someone's vested interests and, therefore, is inherently divisive – from the sort of anti-monotheistic attitude and anti-Abrahamic ethic to which Imam Rauf alludes?

On page 31 of *What's Right With Islam,* Imam Rauf maintains that:

"What is right about any religion or societal structure is therefore the extent to which individuals and

societies fully manifest the principles of the
Abrahamic ethic".

Just prior to the foregoing conclusion, he lists a number of failings of the Muslim community in this respect after the Prophet Muhammad (peace be upon him) passed away – namely, the disappearance of the rule of law applied by an independent judiciary; the judgment that apostasy is the equivalent of treason; continuation of the practice of slavery despite the many Quranic verses that sought to eliminate that institution; and, the on-going oppression of women.

Today, many of these same failings noted with respect to the Muslim community following the passing away of the Prophet Muhammad (peace be upon him) exist in America. For instance, people on both the left and right indicate that the rule of law has been lost amidst a politicizing of the judiciary that has undermined the capacity of the latter to render decisions that are truly independent of political corruption, biases, and agendas. Furthermore, in the post-9/11 environment there are many people who believe that any criticism of a government that systematically oppresses not only its own citizens, but, as well, the populations of other countries on the basis of delusional, self-serving systems of grandiosity and imperialistic greed constitute not only an act of treason but also gives expression to apostasy with respect to the state religion known as the 'war on terror' – where terror is always a function of the atrocities and injustices that others commit and, by definition, never a function of the atrocities and injustices that we commit. In addition, America is filled with people who have become thoroughly enslaved by transnational corporations, money-changers (now known as banks, financial institutions, and the Federal Reserve) whom Jesus (peace be upon him) opposed, and politicians/business people who do not believe that workers ought to be paid fairly or who do not believe that the health and bodily well-being of workers ought to be protected in the workplace, or who do not believe that there is anything wrong with continuing to degrade the environment so that the powerful, wealthy friends of politicians can become more powerful and more wealthy. Finally, America's cup runneth over when it comes to the oppression of women through rape, sexual abuse, authoritarian husbands (as well as fathers and brothers), and the denial of equal opportunity in education, government, and the workplace to women.

How does one compare the extent to which America does not fully manifest the Abrahamic ethic with the extent to which Muslim countries do not fully manifest the Abrahamic ethic, when, in truth, both are failing in major ways? The fact that one country might have a hypothetical score of 30 relative to the hypothetical score of 20 for another country (with a perfect score being 100) is not something about which either country ought to take satisfaction.

Imam Rauf believes that:

"The challenge still facing human society today is how to worship God without dividing ourselves and how to institutionalize such a unified understanding. (page 32)"

Imam Rauf feels that the way to meet this challenge is through a radical monotheism that entails both loving God with all one's being, as well as, establishing a love for others that is equal to the love we have for ourselves and through this love ensure that all human beings enjoy liberty, equality, social justice, and fraternity.

I know of a couple in which the man continuously abused his wife for decades in all manner of ways. Yet, this man was convinced that he loved his wife and that no one would or could love that woman like he did in his own inimitable style.

The woman was not free. She had no semblance of equality of treatment. There was an almost complete absence of justice in the relationship, and there was little, real sense of mutuality and reciprocity that bonded the two.

However, despite the many abusive dimensions of the relationship, the man believed that everything that was done revolved around his supposed love for his wife, and the wife was pushed into such a deep dissociative condition through the presence of the husband's abuse that she came to believe that deep down, beneath all the abuse, was a loving, caring man who had genuine regard for her well-being. Such is the nature of many abusive relationships.

There are many politicians and government officials who act abusively and oppressively toward the citizens of a given country or state, and the politicians and government officials have deluded themselves into believing they are acting out of intentions such as love, compassion, justice, and fairness that supposedly promote the 'greater good' when, in truth, only the good of the relative few are being advanced and served by the agendas of the politicians and governments. There are many citizens who have been pushed so far into a dissociative condition by the presence of such abuse that they can be induced into believing that everything is being done for their (the citizen's) good.

For example, if you make people sufficiently afraid, and if you lie to them about the reasons why they should be afraid, and if you provide them with an identifiable source toward which to direct that fear, then, in the eye of this category 5 hurricane of fear, almost anything the government does to further oppress the citizens can be couched in terms of actions taken to save the citizens from being hurt by the alleged source of fear – a fear that in many, if not most, ways has been manufactured via fabrications and a distorted re-framing of historical and social circumstances. Abusive political relationships exhibit many of the characteristics, themes, and techniques of abusive personal relationships like the husband and wife couple I used to know.

Similarly, just as we often delude ourselves into believing that we love others as we love ourselves, so, too, we often delude ourselves into believing that we love God with our whole being. All too many of us profess a love for God that is really rooted in a desire to have a comfortable material life on Earth, or rooted in a desire for Paradise, or rooted in a fear of Hell, or rooted in a sense of self-glorification related to the presumptuous belief that we are God's elite or chosen emissaries.

There is a story that arises out of the Sufi mystical tradition that runs along the following lines. God says: I created men and they were bound to Me, and they were coming to me when I showed them the world, 9/10ths of them became world-bound, and 1/10th remained with Me. When I told them about Paradise, 9/10ths of those who had remained with Me desired Paradise and only 1/10th remained with Me. When I poured My troubles and My pains upon those who stayed with Me, they cried for help and 9/10ths left and 1/10th remained with Me. And when I threatened those who remained with Me that I would heap upon them such troubles as would make the mountains crumble, they said: "As long as it comes from You it is alright with us".

This latter 1/10th of 1/10th of 1/10th of the original set of human beings are those who love God with their whole being. The Qur'an describes these kinds of individuals in the following way: "Those who spend their wealth for increase in self-purification and have in their minds no favor from anyone for which a reward is expected in return, but only the desire to seek for the Countenance of their Lord Most High." (92: 18-20) And, again: "Say: Surely, my prayer and my service of sacrifice, my life and my death are all for Allah, the Lord of the worlds." (6: 162)

Elsewhere the Qur'an states:

"They ask thee (O Muhammad) what they ought to spend in the way of God. Say: that which is left after meeting your needs." (2: 219)

Many people fulfill this Divine directive by expanding the nature of needs exponentially and reducing what is left over to be spent in the way of Allah proportionately. Their love for God is modulated and limited by the desires of the self and what is meant by loving God with one's whole being is re-framed to refer only to that portion of being that, on occasion, we might loan out in a temporary manner – and assuming, of course, that such a loan is largely free of difficulties and complications.

Contrary to what Imam Rauf asserts, many of us have not just forgotten to apply what we know. Rather, we have forgotten what it means to love God with our whole being. We have forgotten what it means to truly love another human being. We have forgotten the real meaning of liberty, freedom, social justice, and fraternity. We live in a state of spiritual amnesia from which we desperately need to recover.

On pages 35 and 36 of *What's Right With Islam* Imam Rauf outlines five principles that he believes are at the heart of all "globalized' religions – that is, those traditions that were brought to humankind worldwide through the locus of manifestation of authentic prophets and messengers of Divinity. The very first principle concerns the transcendent, singular, unique, unknowable nature of God.

However, God is not only transcendent, God is also immanent. By definition, we cannot know those dimensions of Divinity that are transcendent and unknowable except in a general, referential manner that does nothing more than acknowledge the existence of such realms in relation to the nature of Divinity. Nevertheless, there are facets of Divine Presence that are <u>not unknowable</u> and are capable of, to a degree, being understood according to one's God-given capacity to gain insight into such dimensions of Divinity together with a need for the Divine Grace that renders such realms accessible to our capacities for knowing them.

In addition, I'm not quite certain in what way saying that God is unknowable and transcendent – however true this might be – can be considered a primary, essential principle of 'globalized' religion.

What does one do with such a statement? What practical ramifications does it have?

Once one says that God is unknowable and transcendent, then that is the end of the matter. Everything else is merely ignorance.

Transcendence and unknowability, without a countervailing immanence, is a virtually useless piece of understanding. In fact, one can't even call the former knowledge since to contend that something is unknowable and transcendent means that the statement is entirely unverifiable ... this is the essential nature of being unknowable and transcendent.

The second 'globalized' principle cited by Imam Rauf alludes, somewhat elliptically, to the foregoing issue of immanence. More specifically, he states that "God as All-Being is relevant to His Creation." Through Creation, God provides us with our raison d'être for being by means of the purpose, norms, and ethics toward which human beings are to aspire in the living of life. According to Imam Rauf, God is "the one through whom we learn to know right from wrong."

In concert with a point made previously in the current essay, if God is the One "through whom we learn right from wrong" then distinguishing between right and wrong is not merely a matter of looking into one's heart or conscience and reading off the message of fitra as Imam Rauf seemed to suggest earlier in the first chapter of his book. One has to be taught discernment by Divinity.

Moreover, even if one agrees that God is the One Who provides us with purpose, norms, and ethics, there is a great deal of disagreement about precisely what such purpose, norms and ethics entail. If, as Imam Rauf asserts – and I do not disagree with him on this point – that "God is the most important thing in our lives", questions still hover about the issue of what this all means. People can agree, in principle, that Divinity is relevant to our lives and still disagree about the nature of this relevancy or how one goes about realizing and integrating such relevancy into lived life.

Is the purpose of life to achieve Paradise and avoid Hell? Is the purpose of life to realize the full potential of fitra (our primordial spiritual capacity) quite independently of considerations of Heaven and Hell? Is the purpose of life to realize fitra so that we can come to know and observe, for the very first time in our lives, what worshiping Divinity is really all about in essence? Is the purpose of life to satisfy the Hadith Qudsi that stated that 'God was a Hidden Treasure and loved to be known, so God brought forth Creation'? Is the purpose of life some combination of the foregoing, and, if so, what is the nature of the appropriate sort of combinatorial balance?

How does one go about accomplishing any of the foregoing purposes? What methods are to be used? What criteria are to be applied in evaluating how well, or poorly, one is doing with respect to the realization of any given purpose? How does one interact with others along the way who might be seeking quite different purposes and, yet, still believe that such purposes are divinely ordained? What does it mean to love one's neighbor in such a context?

The third principle of 'globalized' religion to be noted by Imam Rauf is that the nature of the aforementioned Divine relevance is knowable to humans through any of three modalities – taken separately or in combination. These are: (1) divination that is done through various modes of 'seeing' via appropriate states of consciousness and internal spiritual faculties; (2) science and history that consist of the collected knowledge that accumulates in relation to humankind and nature; (3) prophecy that is described as "direct revelation of the will of God through words for the ready use of human understanding."

Any divination that does not take place in a context that is fully modulated by a prophetic mission is problematic. As the Sufi master, Hazrat Junayd (may Allah be pleased with him), stated: This knowledge of ours [that is, Sufi knowledge] is delimited by the Qur'an and the sunnah (i.e., conduct of the Prophet).

Consequently, transpersonal or altered states of consciousness are not necessarily enough, in and of themselves, to ensure that what is being manifested in such states is necessarily an expression of authentic spiritual knowledge of some kind. This is true for the Islamic spiritual tradition, and, as well, I believe authentic spiritual guides from any spiritual tradition would agree that not everything that glitters in the way of divination is necessarily 'gold'. One needs to differentiate veridical spiritual experiences from those that might be generated through the ego, fantasy, Satanic suggestion, psychological problems, and delusional thinking.

Secondly, without wishing to dismiss or discount the value of rigorous, sound, insightful scholarship in the areas of science and history, the fact of the matter is that both science and history have been, and currently are, of limited value when it comes to uncovering the nature of Divinity's relevance to human beings. To be sure, there are many speculations rising out of the mists of quantum physics, evolution, astrophysics, and psychology concerning the origins, meaning, and purpose of life – but that's just what they are ... flights of speculation that, however interesting, intriguing and thought-provoking these might be, they cannot be proven to be true statements about the nature, purpose, and relevance of Divinity to humanity. In fact, many scientists would take umbrage with any attempt to try to forge a bridge between Divinity and humankind via science. To paraphrase Jesus (peace be upon him) 'render unto science the things that are science's and render unto Divinity the things that are God's.'

Of course, some would wish to argue that if there is no reality but God, then in part at least, the subject matter of science does engage Divinity whether scientists acknowledge this or not. From here it is just a skip, hop, and jump to saying that, in principle, science has the capacity to discover various facets of Divinity's relevance to humankind.

There is, however, an assumption implicit in the foregoing line of reasoning. This assumption is that the methods, techniques and processes of science are fully capable of penetrating into, illuminating, and grasping all dimensions of the relation of relevancy between Divinity and humankind.

The realm of the spirit and the nature of the Divine relevancy in human affairs might not necessarily be a function of physical, chemical, biological, material, or mathematical processes except in a very tangential or asymptotic sense. If this is so, then science is largely irrelevant to the issue of uncovering the nature of Divine relevancy to human purpose, meaning, norms, and ethics.

In any event, I have not seen any feasible experimental proofs for the aforementioned assumption. But, if it exists, the guy or gal who came up with the solution deserves at least a Nobel Prize for the discovery.

Finally, to try to argue, as Imam Rauf does, that prophecy "is the direct revelation of the will of God through words for the ready use of human understanding" is problematic in a number of ways. To begin with, I believe Imam Rauf's way of characterizing things with respect to the nature of prophecy is far too limited.

Some have said that prophecy consists of 46 parts. Prophecy is more than being a locus of manifestation of God's will through words ... however important this latter aspect might be.

There is a saying among the Sufis that states:

"Do not think that learning comes from discourse. It comes in 'keeping company'."

Baraka, or Divine Grace, is also transmitted through Prophets, and it is, God willing, the presence of this baraka that underscores the importance of 'keeping company' with a prophet or any other species of Divine friend. In fact, one might say that the meaning of God's will as expressed through Divine words might not be properly understood unless that understanding comes about through support in the form of baraka that is transmitted, if God wishes, through a prophet or authorized vicegerent to those who are keeping company with God's appointed emissary.

Another problem inherent in Imam Rauf's way of describing things in conjunction with the medium of prophecy as one of three ways for generating knowledge concerning the nature of the relevancy of God to Creation is that the meanings and purposes of God's words are not always available for the "ready use of human understanding". There often are conditions surrounding the extent to which God's meanings and purposes will be disclosed through the revealed word.

The Qur'an states:

"If you have taqwa [my note - a reverential awareness in relation to God's presence], He will give you discrimination." (8:29)

The same kind of theme appears in 2: 282 of the Qur'an:

"Have taqwa, and God will teach you."

And, again,

"Say (Muhammad): I call to God upon insight. I and whoever follows after me."

Taqwa, discrimination, insight, and being taught by God are all necessary to engage the meanings of the Qur'an. I have heard my shaykh say on a number of occasions that if an individual approaches the Qur'an with the wrong kind of attitude, then the Qur'an closes itself to that individual even though such a person might continue to read the words, and part and parcel of the appropriate attitude is to have taqwa while engaging God's words.

Not everything in the Qur'an is necessarily for ready use by human understanding. As is indicated in the Qur'an:

"O Mankind! Surely you are ever toiling on towards your Lord, painfully toiling, but you shall meet Him ... you shall surely travel from stage to stage. (84: 6, 9)"

Part of this toiling is struggling to understand all that Divinity is saying to us through not only the words of revelation but the Divine mysteries that stand beneath, beyond, between, and all around those words.

Indeed, as the Prophet Muhammad (peace be upon him) is reported to have said:

"Truly, the Qur'an has an outward and an inward dimension, and the latter has its own inward dimension ... and so on up to seven dimensions."

Words might be the locus of manifestation through which revelation outwardly manifests itself in its most exoteric form, but the reality of revelation might extend into esoteric dimensions that transcend the limits of words:

"We raise by grades of (Mercy) whom We will, and over every lord of knowledge, there is one more knowing. (Qur'an 12: 76)"

The fourth principle of 'globalized religion' mentioned in *What's Right With Islam* revolves around the idea that human beings have the capacity to act in accordance with Divine imperatives. Because human beings have been granted free will, we can choose to act in a manner that is in concert with our knowledge of Divine imperatives and, thereby, do good while avoiding evil. "God has made nature subservient to us." (p. 36)

Human beings also have a capacity to rebel against Divine imperatives. The Qur'an indicates:

"Truly, the soul commands unto evil." (12: 53)

In addition, the Qur'an states:

"Lo! We have placed all that is on the earth as an ornament thereof that We may try them – which of them is best in conduct." (18: 7)

As existentialist philosophers have long noted, one of the primary burdens of life is not only having to choose but to choose in a manner that might be characterized as being "authentic" ... in a way that has moral integrity. One of the companions of the Prophet Muhammad (peace be upon him) gave expression to this essential challenge when he saw a leaf that had fallen from a tree and wished he could be that leaf so that he would not have to carry the burden of choice.

Contrary to what Imam Rauf argued earlier in the Chapter entitled "Common Roots", we do not just suffer from a kind of forgetfulness in which we fail -- due to a lapse in awareness or attention -- to act in accordance with what we know to be appropriate, just, right, or correct, but, as well, we also suffer from the nightmarish condition in which we often know what is right but choose to do otherwise despite what we know. We look Divinity straight in the face and brazenly choose to act in accordance with that within us that commands us to evil ... whether this be the soul, Iblis (Satan), the attraction of the 'ornaments' of creation (dunya), or the encouragement of other rebels who revel in their rebellion against Divinity's Himma or aspiration for humankind.

God has not made nature subservient to human beings. Rather, God has created both human beings and nature with a conditional potential for joining nature and human beings into a relationship of harmony and mutual benefit or disharmony and mutual destruction.

We have the capacity to know. We have the capacity to choose. We have the capacity to act in accordance with Divine preferences. However, we also have the capacity for ignorance, and we have the capacity for evil, and we have the capacity to flout or rebel against Divine preferences.

Nature does not become co-operative with humankind until that individual becomes a sincere servant of Divinity. This is when human beings realize their Divinely-given potential for being God's vicegerents on Earth ... vicegerents who have a fiduciary responsibility to the rest of Creation.

When our internal nature is made subservient to our free will, understanding and actions in relation to Divine preferences, then external nature also becomes consonant with – to the extent that this is possible -- the human being whose spiritual condition is in harmony with Divine wishes. When our internal nature has not been made subservient to Divine preferences through our choosing to exercise free will wisely, then not only is external nature not co-operative with human activity, but external nature actually rebels against human desires – and the environmental problems that have become rampant in every part of the world tends to bear witness to this truth.

One can only oppress nature for so long before its own form of insurgency begins. This is as true for internal nature as it is true for external nature, and the insurgency of our internal world is often manifested in the form of spiritual, physical, and psychological problems.

Imam Rauf believes that human beings know what the Divine preferences are. Even given the presence of Divine revelation in sacred books such as the Qur'an, the Gospel of Jesus (peace be upon him), the Torah of Moses (peace be upon him), and the Psalms of David (peace be upon him), I'm not so sure that human beings do know or understand what God's preferences for human beings are.

For example, a great deal of attention is given in the Muslim community to the five pillars of Islam – namely, (1) bearing witness that there is no god but God and that Muhammad is the Messenger of God; (2) saying prayers five times a day at the appointed times; (3) observing the requirements of fasting during the month of Ramazan; (4) giving zakat or charity based on a percentage of one's accumulated wealth, and (5) performing Hajj or pilgrimage to Mecca and surrounding areas at least once in one's life if one is financially and physically able to do so.

All of the foregoing pillars are important activities to keep in mind, and I have no wish to denigrate such practices. Indeed, I find that, by the Grace of Allah, such activities both help to order my life in constructive and valuable ways, as well as to spiritually strengthen me and, thereby, have enabled me to pursue horizons beyond just the five pillars.

The five pillars are part of the deen or method of spirituality, but there is much more to deen than the five pillars – and by this I do not mean to suggest that the rest of deen is about religious law as conceived of by theologians, legal scholars, and the five schools of Muslim jurisprudence. In fact, in many ways, I find Muslim law as traditionally conceived to be not only largely irrelevant to what I believe Divine preferences to be for human beings, but, as well, often constitutes a major set of obstacles in the way of ever realizing such Divine preferences.

The Qur'an discusses qualities such as patience, love, gratitude, sincerity, integrity, equality, equitability, righteousness, piety, humility, remembrance, insight, forbearance, forgiveness, harmony, balance, honesty, origins, the structure of human nature, nobility, courage, perseverance, striving, struggle, trust, dependence on Divinity, purifying the carnal soul, stations of the heart, human potential, Grace, wisdom, faith, purpose, models of excellence, identity, healing, reflection, character, ethics, opposition to oppressiveness, and much more. I do not find much consideration of these issues during discussions of Muslim law, and, yet, there is roughly 12 times as much exploration of the foregoing topics in the 6000-plus verses of the Qur'an than there is of the 500, or so, verses concerning issues such as inheritance, marriage, divorce, and other like matters that occupy most of the pages of Muslim legal theory.

Is it important to establish boundaries for matters such as marriage, divorce, and inheritance? Yes, it is, but so is learning to develop moral and spiritual character – qualities that not only transcend traditional approaches to the five pillars as well as Muslim systems of jurisprudence but qualities that actually serve to significantly enhance the quality of life of a community, state, or country.

The Prophet Muhammad (peace be upon him) is reported to have said:

"Shall I not inform you about a better act than fasting, charity, and prayer? ... making peace between one another. Enmity and malice tear up heavenly rewards by the root."

Here is something – namely, making peace -- which is described as being better than three of the pillars of Islam, and, yet, many Muslims tend to judge other Muslims on the basis of the latter's observance, or lack thereof, in relation to the five pillars rather than on the basis of a willingness of individuals to try to bring peace to troubled relationships and community.

Another statement that is attributed to the Prophet Muhammad (peace be upon him) is the following:

"God Almighty is the sustainer of people. Among them God loves best those who are of most benefit to others."

Another saying attributed to the Prophet Muhammad (peace be upon him) is the following:

"The Creation is as God's family, for its sustenance is from God. Therefore, the most beloved of God is the person who does good to God's family."

The Prophet is also reported to have asked and answered:

"Do you love your Creator? Then, love your fellow-beings first."

Declaring Shahadah (bearing witness to God's Oneness and the Prophetic mission of Muhammad – peace be upon him), prayer, fasting, and pilgrimage (four of the five pillars of Islam) might, if God wishes, help the individual, but they do not necessarily help the community or the rest of humankind. Naturally, if such activities enable an individual to become a better person then, indirectly, such personal observances might be of assistance to the community if those activities become catalytic agents for an individual to undertake various forms of community work – but this is not always the case.

Nevertheless, an injunction to strive to benefit other people is not, strictly speaking, one of the five pillars of Islam. To be sure, zakat or charity is a spiritual obligation that does carry direct benefit to the needy of society. However, not only is zakat described in the Qur'an as a way of purifying one's wealth and, therefore, is often pursued by human beings for its capacity to render benefit to the individual who is observing this practice rather than primarily for the manner in which it is intended to distribute wealth to those who are less fortunate, but the unfortunate fact of the matter is that many people seek to satisfy only the minimum conditions of zakat and, as a result, do not seek to struggle with the question of whether, or not, there might be a lot more that could do with one's talents and resources in the way of charitable activity than is required by the letter of the law with respect to this pillar of Islam.

In short, all too many people might be content to observe only minimalist Islam with respect to the issue of charity rather than pursue the spirit of the principles inherent in zakat. Consequently, it is quite possible to comply with this pillar of Islam and still be largely disconnected from being committed to helping to alleviate the needs and problems that exist in a given community.

By emphasizing the five pillars of Islam, the impression is often given – by theologians, imams, mullahs, jurists, and Muslim legal scholars -- that these pillars constitute <u>the</u> deen of Islam. This is only partially true, and what is often entirely missing or de-emphasized in such a reductionistic approach to Islam is the significance of a development of

215

the qualities of character that are every bit as important as – if not more so in certain respects -- the five pillars.

The Prophet Muhammad (peace be upon him) is reported to have said:

"I have been given all the Divine Names, and I have been sent to perfect good conduct."

Good conduct entails more than just the five pillars. The Prophet was asked:

"Which part of faith is most excellent?" The Prophet was reported to have replied: "A beautiful character."

On another occasion, the Prophet is reported to have stated:

"The most perfect of the faithful in faith is the most beautiful of them character."

The Prophet is also reported to have said:

"Allah has 300 attributes, and he who acquires just one of these for his own character trait will inherit Paradise."

A beautiful character is more than observing the five pillars. A beautiful character is more than observing the five pillars with ihsan or spiritual excellence.

Furthermore, as the saying attributed to the Prophet noted in the last two lines of the paragraph immediately preceding the above paragraph suggests, there might be ways to Paradise, if God wishes, that are quite independent of the five pillars. Indeed, as Shaykh Abd al-Qadr (may Allah be pleased with him) intimated:

"I did not reach Allah by standing up at night, nor by fasting in the day, nor by studying knowledge. I reached Allah by generosity and humility and soundness of heart."

Does a beautiful character arise out of observance of the five pillars? Although this might be the case for some individuals, it is not necessarily the case for everyone.

The Prophet Muhammad is reported to have said:

"Many are there among you who fast and, yet, gain nothing from it except hunger and thirst, and there are many among you who pray throughout the night and, yet, gain nothing except wakefulness."

One might easily extrapolate this warning to the manner in which some people observe the other pillars of Islam.

For some, and, perhaps, for many, the lessons of: humility, gratitude, dependence, love, sincerity, perseverance, honesty, nobility equitability, generosity, integrity, courage, forbearance, forgiveness, and friendliness arise out of engaging the trials and tribulations of life that take place quite independently of the five pillars. The Qur'an indicates:

"Lo! Ritual worship preserves one from lewdness and iniquity, but, verily, remembrance of Allah is more important" (29: 45),

and remembrance of God's Presence according to the multiplicity of Names and Attributes of Divinity through which Divinity interacts with Creation is one of the primary ingredients in the formation of character amidst the trials of life ... trials that God has placed into our lives for just this purpose. Remembrance puts things in perspective.

As the Qur'an informs us:

"We have created life and death that We may try which of you is best in conduct. He is the Mighty, the Forgiving." (67: 2)

And, again, as indicated previously, conduct extends far beyond the five pillars and/or the legalistic prescriptions of this or that school of law.

All of the foregoing discussion about character or akhlaq and the ways in which character cannot necessarily be subsumed under, or neatly reduced, to the five pillars of Islam is intended to be juxtaposed next to Imam Rauf's belief that Muslims <u>know</u> what Divinity's preferences are for humankind. The questions that arise as a result of this sort of juxtaposition is especially pointed when all too many Muslim jurists, mullahs, imams, educators, and legal scholars use undue influence (in mosques, madrassas -- schools, Muslim gatherings, and the media) to re-frame the nature of those preferences and, in many ways, deflect attention away from and/or restrict the interpretation of such Divine preferences to purely legal matters as understood by traditional theories of Muslim law.

Imam Rauf might agree with many of the foregoing points. But, if he does, then this agreement sits in opposition, to some degree, with his contention that Muslims know what Divinity's preferences are for human kind.

Contrary to what Imam Rauf seems to suppose, I feel (based on those with whom I have interacted over some thirty-five years across four continents, as well as based on the books, articles, and lectures by a variety of Muslim authors upon which I have reflected) there seem to be a lot of Muslims who are confused about what the Divine preferences are for humankind. I also believe that a lot of this confusion is due to the misinformation and misunderstanding that is fed to them by so-called religious leaders in a pervasive pattern of spiritual abuse that is oppressively imposed from a very early age – both informally and formally.

The fifth and last principle to be listed by Imam Rauf as basic to any 'globalized' religion through which human beings come to understand the nature of Divine relevancy to humankind concerns the idea that human beings are both responsible and to be held accountable for what is done or not done while journeying through the life of this world. Unfortunately, at least in my opinion, he speaks about accountability in terms of reward and punishment.

I have difficulty reconciling Imam Rauf's earlier emphasis on loving "God with all our heart, mind, soul, and strength" (page 18) with the issue of reward and punishment. In fact, juxtaposing the two together seems something of an oxymoron.

Hazrat Abu Bakr Sadiq said:

"The sign of attachment with the Beloved is detachment from all else."

This "all else" includes matters pertaining to reward and punishment. A Sufi saying that is appropriate here states:

"The Lover begs of the Beloved nothing but the Beloved. Accursed is the lover who begs of one's Beloved anything except the Beloved."

To speak of reward and punishment is really to introduce into any discussion of loving God with all one's being elements that pertain to other than a focus on the Beloved.

The Prophet Muhammad (peace be upon him) alluded to something of a similar nature when he is reported to have said:

"This world is prohibited to the people of the next world, and the next world is prohibited to the people of this world, and they are both forbidden to the people of Allah."

The people of God are those who, among other things, love Divinity independently of all considerations of reward and punishment.

'Ishq is an Arabic word that means ardent, intense love. The word is derived from the term 'ashiqa that refers to a plant that twines itself around another plant or small tree and deprives the latter of the sustenance necessary to develop leaves and fruit. Eventually, the deprived entity dries up, turns yellow, and dies.

Shaykh al-Shibli (may Allah be pleased with him) asks the question: "What is love?" and then answers the question.

"Love is like a cup of fire which blazes terribly ... when it takes root in the senses and settles in the heart, it annihilates."

Love is the 'ashika plant that crawls its way into our hearts and being and cuts one off from that which connects us, and sustains that connection, with the material world. Eventually, the one who is captivated by love dies to one self and to the world and passes away into the condition of fana when one's awareness is overwhelmed by the presence of the Beloved and is dead to everything else.

Love is the forging process that leads to spiritual transformation. The dross material of humanity is placed upon the anvil of life to be pounded by the hammer of experience.

The Divine Blacksmith tempers the dross material by alternately placing that material in spiritual conditions of fire (jalali) and water (jamali) before returning that material to the anvil for further pounding from life experience. And, in the end, if God wishes, the dross material is transformed into something of constructive use that has been purified and fortified to meet "the slings and arrows of outrageous fortune" with integrity and character.

None of the foregoing comments concerning love are meant to deny the realities of Heaven and Hell nor to deny those realities that revolve about the possibility of reward and punishment. However, this latter sort of vernacular really does not have much relevance to the topic of love.

In fact, we have arrived at something of a crossroads that underscores one of the fundamental differences between exoteric and esoteric approaches with respect to trying to understand the nature of Divine preferences for human beings. Exoteric approaches to spirituality (and included in this are most of the Muslim legal systems) tend to be rooted in a carrot and stick approach that emphasizes extrinsic techniques of motivation that work -- oftentimes in awkward, unnatural and oppressive ways -- on the human heart from the outside in, whereas esoteric approaches tend to be rooted in the most essential of intrinsic motivations – namely love -- in which spiritual desire and motivation flow from within in a way that is entirely consistent and synergistically resonant with, as well as nurturing to, our primordial spiritual capacity or fitra.

Paul said in 2 Corithinians 3: 6:

'The letter of the law killeth but the spirit giveth life.'

When I hear Muslims speak proudly about how they believe that Islam is the fastest growing religion in the world, I also think about how, in many ways, Islam is also the fastest dying religion in the world because soon after proclaiming the Shahadah that there is no god but God and Muhammad is the messenger of God, I see many of these newcomers initiated into a system of spiritual abuse in which idols are made of this or that theology or this and that Muslim legal system, as well as this or that traditional form of taqlid (blind obedience).

Taqlid is an Arabic word that is derived from a root that refers to a collar or restraint that is intended to control something – for example, an animal. Far too many Muslims are rendered into beasts of burden whose imposed duty is to carry the theological and legal baggage of all too many imams, mullahs, jurists, legal scholars, Muslim leaders, and theologians ... beasts of burden who are threatened with the whip of hell-fire if they do not do as their idol-masters demand while simultaneously being seduced with come hither whisperings and endearments of a Paradise that often has been sadly and pathetically reduced to sexual pleasures even as God is forgotten.

Rather than attempting to delineate the essence of what has been taught by all authentic prophets worldwide and across history in the manner in which Imam Rauf has done on pages 35 and 36 of *What's Right With Islam*, I would offer the following alternative way of saying things. This way is, I believe, a way that is fully consonant with the spiritual teachings brought by the authentic emissaries of Divinity.

Life is rooted in self-awareness and the awareness of experience. Out of these several forms of awareness arise curiosity and questions concerning the significance of the contents of awareness. These questions revolve around issues of: identity, purpose, meaning, values, suffering, well-being, methods, and truth. In conjunction with these questions various kinds of intentions and choices emerge that begin to engage such themes according to personal predilections. All choices, no matter what they might be, entail struggle and striving. Out of these efforts various kinds of insight, interpretation, reflection, understanding, and judgment emanate in relation to the questions of life and the contents of consciousness. We act on or apply these understandings in emotional, psychological, worldly, or spiritual ways, and what we do will be evaluated ... by ourselves, by others, and by the nature of what is.

All of the foregoing is measured against the degree to which the process of life gives expression to or conforms to the truth, as well as the extent to which justice is done to that truth in relation to each and every facet of our awareness, experience, choice, struggling, understanding, doing, and evaluating. Truth and justice are set by that which is independent of human construction, and it is the task of human existence to merge horizons with such truth and justice according to our capacity to do so. To the extent that one is successful in fully realizing one's capacity for truth and justice, then to this extent does one come to know, love, and worship the nature of Divine relevancy to humankind ... to this extent does one develop character ... to this extent does one come to know, if God wishes, the Hidden Treasure that Divinity loved to be known ... to this extent does one fulfill one's spiritual destiny.

Toward the latter part of Chapter One in *What's Right With Islam*, Imam Rauf titles the final section of that chapter in the following way: 'Jews and Christians: Siblings On The Block'. Imam Rauf cites a Quranic verse that informs Muslims that they should "not argue with the People of the Book except in the best way" (2: 62) When reading this verse, I am struck by the thought – as I am sure many Jews and Christians are struck by the thought – that suicide bombings probably don't capture the essence of what Divine guidance is getting at here.

A little further down the page in relation to the relationship among, on the one hand, Jews and Christians, and, on the other hand, Muslims, Imam Rauf states the following:

"Disagreement between them certainly exists, but all disagreements are no more than family disputes".

While reading the foregoing quote I was struck by the idea – as I am sure many other Muslims are struck

226

– that reducing Lebanon, Palestine, and Iraq to rubble while killing, maiming, and torturing tens of thousands of the inhabitants of these countries appears to be something more than a "family feud", "disagreement", or some other well-chosen euphemism. Imam Rauf must have attended the same school as did those who came up with the terms of "collateral damage" and "extreme rendition" as civilized ways of talking about murder, kidnapping, and torture.

Toward the bottom of page 37 of *What's Right With Islam* Imam Rauf says:

"The Quran did criticize the Jews for failure to uphold the Torah (5: 68-70) for excessive legalism and exaggerated authoritarianism by some of the rabbis (3: 50, 5: 66-68) and for nationalizing monotheism (2: 111)."

However, what Imam Rauf does not state is how Muslims should be criticized for failing to uphold the revealed scriptures that were given to them, or for the excessive legalism and exaggerated authoritarianism of various imams, mullahs, theologians, leaders, and jurists, or for the way in which Saudi Arabia, Afghanistan, Pakistan, Kuwait, Iran, and other Muslim localities have sought to nationalize Islamic monotheism ... and similar things could be said in criticism of Christians for committing precisely the same kinds of error.

On page 39 of *What's Right With Islam*, Imam Rauf indicates that the Qur'an praises Christians in various ways and declares Christians closest to Muslims because of "their warm practice of neighborly love." I'm sure that all the peoples in Central America, South America, the Middle East, Africa, Vietnam and the rest of Asia who have been oppressed and exploited by imperialist, colonialist, and capitalist strains of Christianity across history – including today -- would fully concur with the foregoing.

Every spiritual, economic, political, and philosophical tradition is populated by both Cains and Ables. The Ables of the world – whether they be Muslim, Jewish, Christian, Buddhist, Hindu, Jain, Taoist, Aborigine, Maori, some form of indigenous spirituality from the Western Hemisphere, or humanists – they try to observe a "warm practice of neighborly love" to one another – even to the Cains ... whereas the Cains of the world – whether they be so-called Muslim, Jewish, Christian, humanist, and so on – tend not to observe a "warm practice of neighborly love" to anyone, including themselves.

According to Imam Rauf, we – Jews, Muslims, and Christians – are basically:

"All right as long as we believe in the one God, try to love God as best we can, and make our best effort in treating humanity humanely."

And, this is so he believes in spite of whatever mistakes we might have made in our understanding of Divinity and in our practical observance of such understanding.

The problem with the foregoing is that we continue to make mistakes with respect to the nature of Divinity, what it means to love God, or how to treat humanity humanely. Consequently, things are not all right, and events around the world are screaming this at the top of their lungs … events for which Muslims, Jews, Christians, Hindus, Buddhists, the practitioners of many other spiritual traditions, and humanists bear the fullest of responsibility.

The Prophet Muhammad (peace be upon him) is reported to have asked the people with him:

"What actions are most excellent?" And, then, he is reported to have provided the following answer: "To gladden the heart of a human being; to feed the hungry; to help the afflicted; to lighten the sorrow of the sorrowful, and to remove the wrongs of the injured."

There is nothing in the foregoing saying that is restricted in its scope with respect to humankind. These actions are most excellent no matter who performs them and no matter in relation to whom they are performed.

-----

6) Open Letter to Feisal Rauf & Daisy Khan

(With a few minor changes, the following letter is, essentially, the same e-mail that was sent to, and received by, Feisal Rauf and Daisy Khan on August 23, 2010.)

The intention with which I write this letter is as a friend – although I realize that you might not consider me to be a friend. After all, I have been publically critical of Feisal's book: *What's Right With Islam*. However, if friends can't be honest with one another, then, I'm not really sure what friendship means.

Moreover, we previously have sat down face-to-face on a number of occasions to break bread and discuss issues of importance. I might not always have said what you liked or stated that with which you agreed, but I have always interacted with you both in a sincere fashion.

I once asked you, Daisy, to look in on a friend and her two children because I was concerned about their physical and spiritual welfare given that they seemed to be inextricably entangled with a fraudulent Sufi teacher. I asked you to do this because, among other reasons, you were relatively proximate to, and a friend of, the family in question while I was living more than ten hours travel-time away from them, and because -- for reasons about which you were cognizant -- a phone call from me might not have been well received.

You expressed mystification about what I believed you could do concerning those three individuals, and I said: "Be a Friend". In response you said during our phone conversation that you were planning to meet with the mother in the near future, and you indicated to me you would try to gauge what was going on. I assume this was done – I have to assume this since I never heard back from you on the matter.

I also have tried to get in touch with Feisal on several occasions – both by e-mail and phone. On one of these occasions, I spoke with you and asked you to pass on a message to Feisal that I wanted to talk with him about an issue of some importance to me.

Once again, I never heard back. So, I have to assume that neither of you consider me to be a friend despite our past relatively, friendly interactions.

I can't do anything about your side of the situation. All I can try to do is look after my own spiritual condition.

I have never written either of you off. I did not do this despite my disappointment in some of the things you were saying and doing – such as Feisal's support for the fatwa that tried to justify Muslims killing other Muslims in Iraq and Afghanistan ... a fatwa that Feisal sent to *The New York Times* encouraging them to publish it and that was included in Feisal's book (*What's Right With Islam*) – a position that I publically criticized on a number of occasions.

On the other hand, you both have been giving me some fairly clear signals for quite some time that you did not wish to have anything to do with me. Consequently, I consider our relationship to be one of estrangement – that is, something which is, in a sense, still open, in however a tenuous manner, but fraught with tension of one kind or another and something that might never get resolved.

In any case, despite the turbulent waters that have flowed beneath the existential bridge so elusively connecting us, I am currently writing to you both as a friend. Moreover, what I have to say now is from nowhere but my heart and soul with a deep concern for your spiritual welfare, as well as the welfare of all Americans and people throughout the world.

You, Feisal, have been criticized by, among others, Newt Gingrich for claiming that the United States was, in a sense, partially responsible for what happened on 9/11. Your position is the 'blowback' theory championed by a variety of people – including Noam Chomsky, Chalmers Johnson, Amy Goodman, and the late Howard Zinn – that through the oppressive and destructive policies conducted by the United States government in relation to many Muslim countries over the last six decades (starting, perhaps, with the CIA's over-throw of the legally elected Mossadegh's government in Iran in 1953), the **234** United States incited various elements in the Muslim world to get revenge against the United States ... revenge which allegedly came home to roost on 9/11.

Your 'blowback' position is in need of revision, for it is inconsistent with the actual facts of 9/11. You should revise your understanding in the light of testimony from, among others: Sibel Edmonds, Indira Singh, Mike Ruppert, Barry Jennings, David Chandler, William Rodriquez, Richard Grove, Robin Wright, Colleen Rowley, April Gallop, David Schippers, Pierre Henry-Brunel, Judy Wood, Kevin Ryan, A.K. Dewdney, Steven Jones, Anthony Shaffer, Richard Gage, William Lagasse and Chadwick Brooks (both of the latter individuals are Pentagon Police Officers), as well as hundreds of architects, engineers, scientists, pilots (both commercial and military), fire-fighters (including the first responders whose testimony was finally released under a Freedom of Information suit by the New York Times against the City of New York), ex-CIA officers, and workers at both Arlington Cemetery and the Naval Annex who have come forth with evidence that collectively demonstrates that the "official" conspiracy theory concerning 9/11 cannot withstand critical scrutiny – in other words, that what is alleged to have happened, among other places, at the Twin Towers and the Pentagon did not occur in the way that has been claimed in: *The 9/11 Commission Report*; the various NIST

(National Institute of Standards and Technology) reports concerning the Twin Towers and Building 7; or, the *Pentagon Performance Report.*

235

John Farmer, who headed up one of the 9/11 Commission research teams, has indicated that there were many dynamics taking place behind the scenes of the Commission that ensured Philip Zelikow -- a person with deep ties and conflicts of interest concerning the Bush Administration (conflicts of interest about which he remained silent when he was being interviewed for the position of: 'Director of the 9/11 Commission') -- had complete control over what did and did not see the light of day during the investigation. Not only is there evidence to indicate that Zelikow had already written a first draft of the Commission's Report prior to any witnesses being deposed, but there also is overwhelming evidence to indicate that Zelikow actively sought to exclude important testimony from the investigatory and reporting process by preventing many, if not all, of the testimony from the foregoing listed names to be properly considered or openly discussed through the public hearings that took place in conjunction with the work of the 9/11 Commission.

I believe you are honorable people who are seeking to do good as best you currently are able to understand what that might mean and involve. I believe your Cordoba initiative is done with such an intention.

I do not believe you are willfully holding an opinion concerning the events of 9/11 that is contrary to the facts. Rather, I believe you hold the opinion you do because you are ignorant of the actual facts – because you either have not had the time or taken the time to do due diligence with respect to conducting rigorous research concerning 9/11.

I believe your situation vis-à-vis 9/11 is that of many Americans and even that of many people in the media. I do not believe any of you are part of some vast conspiracy to cover up the truth about 9/11.

I believe you have made the same mistake that many people have committed in this matter. You have let other people provide you with many of your opinions and ideas about 9/11 without bothering to properly verify or vet those sources.

Based solely on your public statements (such as, among other places, your book: *What's Right With Islam*), I know that you have not carefully, if at all, gone through *The 9/11 Commission Report*, The FEMA Report, the NIST reports, or the *Pentagon Performance Report*. I know with even more certainty that you have not taken the time to listen to the testimony or read the testimony of most, if not all, of the witnesses who I mentioned earlier.

I know this because if you had done such due diligence you would have come to a much different conclusion than you have concerning the events of 9/11. I know this because you have had a good education and, at one point in your life, were heading toward a career in science and, therefore, you are capable of looking at empirical data or experimental results and, then, are able to critically analyze such material in order to evaluate its credibility and viability. I know this because I have had discussions with you previously about technical issues.

The problem, however, is that you really have not looked at the actual data and facts concerning 9/11. Indeed, as indicated, your problem is that of many individuals in America – individuals of good will and decency – who have accepted, without much critical investigation of their own, what other people have had to say about 9/11 ... other people who had positions of responsibility concerning the investigation of 9/11 but, unfortunately, betrayed the American people instead.

I don't know what the motives of such people were. I am not interested in speculating about them.

What I do know is that they got pretty much everything wrong in relation to 9/11. They committed egregious errors of both commission and omission during their inquiries into such things as the collapse of the Twin Towers, the collapse of Building 7, the devastation at the Pentagon, and the jet crash in the field in Pennsylvania.

I have no theory about who, or what, is responsible for the events of 9/11. I have not formed any conclusions -- one way or the other -- whether the alleged 19-20 hijackers actually had anything to do (whether peripherally, indirectly, or directly) with 9/11.

Individuals who demand an answer to the following question [namely, if the 19 or 20 Muslims identified by the FBI as being responsible for 9/11 did not commit the terrorist acts that occurred on that tragic day, then who did?] are, in effect, trying to place the cart before the horse. They are pursuing a mode of logical reasoning that is not likely to get anyone very far if this is to be the point of departure for all ensuing exploratory travel concerning 9/11.

First one needs to establish the facts. Once this has been done, then one needs to connect the dots to see where they lead with respect to the people who might be implicated by those facts.

No one in the government, academia, or the mainstream media has done any of their so-called fact finding in a way that is capable of plausibly demonstrating that the Twin Towers or Building 7 collapsed in the way alleged. No one in the government, academia, or the mainstream media has done any of the necessary fact finding in a manner that is capable of plausibly accounting for what allegedly occurred at the Pentagon. No one in government, academia, or the mainstream media has done any of the required fact finding in a way that plausibly explains what allegedly went on in Shanksville, Pennsylvania.

None of the foregoing is about who is responsible for 9/11. It is entirely about what actually happened – and can be demonstrated – with respect to the <u>physical facts</u> of 9/11.

Why have I bothered to provide the foregoing overview concerning certain facets of 9/11? There are several reasons.

First, I am trying to induce you both to actually take the time to verify whether, or not, your beliefs concerning 9/11 are correct and viable. You cannot do this without going through the physical evidence alluded to before, and, to date, I am certain that you have not done this with much deliberation … if at all.

Secondly, as long as your opinions concerning 9/11 are critically and factually uninformed, you are not really in any position to make sound judgments concerning the present situation vis-à-vis Cordoba House aka Park51, or the so-called Ground Zero Mosque. Pressure is mounting for you and the other stakeholders of SoHo Properties to acquiesce to the demands of many Americans that you should be willing to move your project to another, less sensitive, less problematic location.

Unfortunately, almost everyone is arguing about the wrong principles with respect to the foregoing controversy. The central issue is not about First Amendment rights, nor is it about the right of Americans to have their sensitivities concerning 9/11 be given proper consideration, nor is it about the rights of 9/11 families to be saved from further insult and injury ... although all of these principles are, in their own context, perfectly understandable and not unreasonable.

The real principle at the heart of the 'Cordoba House' controversy is the elephant in the room that no one wants to talk about. The elephant is named "Truth and Justice", and it is the visibly invisible ghost of 9/11.

Three thousand innocents – both Americans and foreign nationals – were assassinated on 9/11. Then, when there was a rush to judgment by all too many people who should have known better, the tragedy of 9/11 led to the further slaughter of tens of thousands of more innocents in Iraq and Afghanistan, along with tens of thousands more who have been maimed for life – both American and non-American and both Muslim and non-Muslim.

In the process, the families of 9/11 victims have been betrayed. The people of America have been betrayed. The soldiers of America have been betrayed. The people of Iraq and Afghanistan have been betrayed. Truth and justice have been betrayed.

How can you or the other stakeholders of SoHo Properties reach an equitable resolution with respect to the Cordoba House controversy when the whole brouhaha is predicated on misinformation and ignorance concerning the facts of the matter of 9/11? Your present controversy cannot be properly resolved, America's 9/11 wounds cannot be adequately healed, and the tremendous injustices inflicted on Iraq and Afghanistan cannot be adequately addressed until the truth about 9/11 is established.

Mark Twain once said: "The trouble with the world is not that people know too little, it's that they know so many things that aren't so." No truer words have ever been said about people's ideas and opinions concerning 9/11.

If 9/11 families and the people of America want their concerns and sensitivities properly taken into consideration with respect to the Cordoba House project, then, they need to reciprocate and take steps to ensure that what they believe to have happened on 9/11 actually took place in the way that the official story claims. For, if things concerning 9/11 are other than they are officially framed to be, the 9/11 families and the people of America will need to adopt an entirely different set of concerns and sensitivities with respect to 9/11.

If anyone would like to interject at this point that the facts of 9/11 already have been established, then they haven't been paying attention to what was said previously. Anyone who has <u>not</u> gone through: *The 9/11 Commission Report,* the NIST reports, *The Pentagon Performance Report,* as well as listened carefully to the testimony of all of the people I have listed earlier (and many others could be added to that list) and who were prevented (either actively or passively) from testifying before the 9/11 Commission – such a person really has no idea of what might, or might not, have taken place on 9/11.

The understanding of such an individual concerning the physical facts of 9/11 has been provided for them through something other than their own due diligence. Anyone who is honest about this issue will admit as much.

Feisal and Daisy, you, and others at SoHo Properties, have an unprecedented opportunity to do great service to both truth and justice, as well as to the 9/11 families, the rest of America, democracy, and the peoples of Iraq and Afghanistan. Actually, there is no one else on the face of the earth at the present time that has the same chance as you now possess to ensure that the right thing is done with respect to so many principles and people.

This opportunity might never come again. You have a chance to do what no one else has been able to achieve with respect to 9/11 -- namely, seek a new investigation into 9/11 that is objective, rigorous, independent, thorough, and capable of generating results that are actually able to reflect the full set of existing data concerning 9/11 ... something that has not, yet, happened through: the government, the media, academia, or any of the organizations that officially have been linked to the supposed official investigation into 9/11.

As an act of good faith, I feel you should be willing to move your Cordoba House project to another location. However, in exchange for your act of good faith you should require a reciprocal act of good faith – an agreement to establish (through state and/or federal grand juries) an exhaustive exploration into 9/11.

In fact, since David Patterson, the governor of New York, has graciously offered to help you find a suitable but alternative location for the Cordoba House project, I propose that David Patterson also has the authority to ensure that an appropriately unbiased grand jury of New Yorkers be convened for the purposes of investigating the murders of 9/11 – just like any other murders that have occurred, or will occur, on New York State soil. The Office of David Patterson would be a natural bridge through which both sides of the offered good faith might meet and reach a just and equitable resolution to the current controversy.

I have confidence in the American people. Moreover, the great work that state and federal grand juries do at least five days a week all across America in helping to protect democracy demonstrates that my faith in the American people is justified.

If a group of average Americans is permitted to investigate 9/11 via a grand jury format and follow the evidence wherever it takes them and subpoena power permits, I believe that the results of such an investigation will be fair and impartial. I believe that when they consider all the relevant evidence they will arrive at a judicious conclusion concerning 9/11.

However, this challenge must be under the full authority of the people of America, not the government. Let the people fulfill the purposes for which grand juries were originally established as the last bastion of defense against forces of tyranny and injustice that are capable of undermining democracy and freedom.

If you have the foresight to adopt and realize the proposal I am making concerning the exchange of location for a proper investigation into 9/11, the entire world will owe you a debt of gratitude. If you have the courage to adopt and realize the proposal I am making, the whole purpose of Cordoba House would have been fulfilled before it was even built.

I will end with some words from a Tracy Chapman song:

Don't be tempted by the shiny apple;

Don't you eat of the bitter fruit;

Hunger only for the taste of justice;

Hunger only for the word of truth,

For all you have is your soul.

As a friend, I can think of no better counsel to give you.

Anab Whitehouse

[To date, I have received no response from either Imam Feisal Rauf or Daisy Khan concerning the foregoing communication to them.]

| Islam and Democracy |

7) Constitutional 911

[The following essay is not a critical examination of specific passages from Imam Rauf's book, *What's Right With Islam*. On the other hand, the material below does explore a wide variety of issues that Imam Rauf touches upon and discusses in his book, and, therefore, the essay has been included in the present collection because it critically engages some of the same terrain as does Imam Rauf's book and, yet, does so from a very different perspective than does Imam Rauf.]

Many people have criticized both *The 9/11 Commission Report* and the various NIST (National Institute of Standards and Technology) reports concerning the collapse of three buildings at Ground Zero in New York for lacking qualities such as: thoroughness, rigor, accuracy, and integrity. What I have not seen to date – although someone, somewhere might have said something on this topic – is that the very processes through which the 9/11 Commission and NIST were permitted to produce their reports were unconstitutional.

In other words, neither the 9/11 Commission nor NIST had constitutional authority to do what they did. More specifically, Congress did not have the Constitutional authority to pass legislation to create the 9/11 Commission, and the Department of Commerce -- the parent body of NIST -- did not have constitutional authority to enable NIST to conduct its research and produce its reports in relation to 9/11.

No matter what one's theory concerning 9/11 might be, I believe there is indisputable evidence that the events of 9/11 have been used as a pretext for eviscerating the Constitution – and, actually, some of these issues [for example, torture, extreme rendition, warrantless wiretaps, the Patriot Act, and undeclared wars) already have been explored and analyzed by a variety of people Yet, many of these same individuals who have been critical of the government in the ways noted previously seem to be of the opinion that although the 9/11 Commission and NIST had the right to do what they did, they just did it badly, and, as a result, such critics seem to have failed to understand that the 9/11 Commission and the NIST reports were part of the Constitutional evisceration process that ensued from 9/11.

Great tragedy occurred on September 11th, 2001. Obviously, the nearly 3000 lives that were lost on 9/11 -- along with the many families that, as a result, were adversely affected -- is near the top of the list.

However, the damage that has been done, and is being done, to the Constitution is enabling many more such tragedies to unfold. The patriot Act, the wars in Iraq and Afghanistan (where hundreds of thousands more people have died), torture, extreme rendition, crimes against humanity, warrantless wiretapping, hundreds of billions of dollars that have been wasted on war, crippling indebtedness, a failing economy – these are all the bastard children of countless incestuous affairs being illicitly conducted (that is, which are unconstitutional) within, and through, the federal government.

The following discussion outlines the underlying issues. In addition, this essay will explore a few of the ramifications that have arisen through the unconstitutional processes at issue.

The Constitutional basis for my contention concerning the 9/11 Commission and NIST are rooted in four provisions of the Constitution and after listing these roots, I will elaborate upon them in greater detail through much of the remainder of this essay. (1) *Article IV, Section 4* of the Constitution states that: "The United States shall <u>guarantee</u> every state in the union, a republican form of government." (2) The *Preamble to the Constitution* stipulates that the purpose for which the Constitution has been created is: "to establish a more perfect union, establish justice, insure domestic tranquility, provide for the common defense, promote the general welfare, and secure the blessings of liberty for ourselves and our posterity." (3) *The Ninth Amendment* indicates that: "The enumeration in the Constitution of certain rights shall not be construed to deny or disparage others retained by the people." (4) The *Tenth Amendment* stipulates that: "The powers not delegated to the United States by the Constitution, nor prohibited to it by the states, are reserved to the states respectively, or to the people."

-----

(1) The promise of republican government in Article IV, Section 4 of the Constitution has nothing to do with the Republican Party. In fact, although I am not a Democrat, nor do I belong to any other political party, nonetheless, one might easily argue – and quite plausibly I believe (and this will be elaborated upon shortly) – that the current Republican Party is the complete antithesis of the actual meaning of "republicanism" being referred to in the Constitution ... although to be fair about the matter, one quite justifiably could say the same thing of the existing Democratic Party – namely, that when its candidates are elected they usually do not properly observe the fiduciary responsibilities that are entailed by a republican form of government.

The idea of guaranteeing every state in the union, a republican form of government could be read in, at least, two ways. (a) The federal government is guaranteeing that every state will have a republican form of government, and, (b) the federal government is guaranteeing that the federal government will provide a republican form of government in its relations with the various states.

Interpretation (a) is both oppressively tyrannical and runs contrary to the whole revolutionary and constitutional history of

America. Therefore, the guarantee of republican government being issued through Article IV, Section 4 is about the quality of government that the central government will offer to each of the states of the union.

Unfortunately, the sad fact of the matter is that almost every administration in the federal government that has taken office since the inception of the United States of America has failed to realize the Constitutional requirements of Article 4, Section 4 – which is not a promise, but a guarantee -- concerning the matter of a republican form of government. Consequently, almost from the very beginning of this country as a constitutionally constructed entity, virtually every federally elected government has conducted its administration in an unconstitutional manner.

When the Constitutional Convention was in progress in Philadelphia, much of the discussion was done through a spirit of republicanism. Indeed, republicanism was part of the ideology of the Enlightenment that influenced the Framers of the Constitution, and, as such, republicanism was: a way of life; a way of thinking; a way of behaving.

Moreover, the theme of republicanism was so close to the hearts of the Framers of the Constitution they held that no one should govern others unless such leaders were completely governed by republican principles. This was so much the case that it was enshrined in the Constitution in Article IV, Section 4, and was probably one of the primary reasons why individuals such as Madison and Monroe initially felt there was no need to create a separate Bill of Rights since the guarantee of republican government contained in the Constitution should – they believed – satisfactorily accommodate such concerns.

So, what is republicanism? It encompasses a set of core values such as: being benevolent; having integrity; demonstrating character; showing judiciousness; displaying egalitarianism; possessing and giving expression to qualities of virtue; being truly disinterested in personal gain or profit while serving others; having the capacity to be impartial arbiters in all matters and, therefore, never serving as a judge in one's own cause; showing tolerance and modesty in all matters; exhibiting unfailing honesty; manifesting honor and reasonableness in every affair; being willing to sacrifice oneself for the good of others; being unbiased and independent when evaluating and judging any situation; having high-mindedness guide one's thoughts and actions in relation to the public good.

In an ideal republican world, a person in government would not receive a salary or profit for one's labors on behalf of the public. This is one of the reasons why many of the individuals who stayed for the entire Constitutional Convention struggled financially throughout the process, and it is also one of the reasons why others who had assembled for the Constitutional Convention had to leave before the process had been completed – namely, they could no longer afford to survive in Philadelphia and be away from their means of generating income.

Given the foregoing set of republican values, one could understand how people like Monroe and Madison believed that a Bill of Rights was unnecessary. After all, if government officials lived in accordance with the requirements of republican values then all of the protections of human rights that are given a voice through the Bill of Rights could be satisfied by individuals who operated through republican values ... or, so, the theory went.

Fortunately, there were many other individuals in the Colonies who, although they admired and sought to abide by the values inherent in the republican spirit, they, nevertheless, had a less sanguine – or, perhaps, more realistic -- view of human potential. They realized that not all individuals who achieved elected or appointed office in the Federal Government could necessarily be counted on to abide by the requirements of a republican philosophy.

Consequently, these more far-sighted members of the fraternity of Framers had the guarantee of republican government written into the Constitution. In addition, they insisted that unless there was a separate Bill of Rights that would be added to the main body of the Constitution very soon after the ratification process had been completed, then there would be no ratification of the Constitution as written ... the issue was, in a sense, a deal-breaker.

The republican spirit prevailed. A gentleman's agreement on the Constitution had been brokered, and soon after the Constitution was ratified, a process for developing a Bill of Rights was instituted, and the results of that process were subsequently ratified in 1791.

Article VI of the Constitution states:

"This Constitution, and the laws of the United States which shall be made in pursuance thereof; and all treaties made, or which shall be made, under the authority of the United States, shall be the supreme law of the land; and the judges in every state shall be bound thereby, anything in the Constitution or laws of any State to the contrary notwithstanding.

"The Senators and Representatives before mentioned and the members of the several state legislatures, and all executive and judicial officers, both of the United States and the several states, shall be bound by oath or affirmation, to support this Constitution."

Among other things, the foregoing excerpt from the Constitution – the beginning portion of that is referred to as 'the Supremacy Clause' –

indicates that all laws must be in compliance with the Constitution. This means, among other things, that all laws must be in compliance with the guarantee of republican government.

In short, one of the primary filters through which everything in the Constitution must be understood is encompassed by the "guarantee of republican government". If one wishes to talk about the intent of the Framers, then everything that they did, said and wrote was a function of republican values and principles because that is the philosophy and understanding that essentially shaped their perspective concerning government and social affairs.

Anything that does not satisfy the guarantee of republican government is unconstitutional. Furthermore, all Senators, Representatives, members of the state legislatures, as well as all executive and judicial officers are bound by the requirements of the guarantee of republican government to acknowledge as much.

Unfortunately, for most of the history of the United States the aforementioned guarantee has not only been unacknowledged, but, as well, it has not been properly enforced with respect to the actions of any of the branches of federal government. Consequently, many of the Congressional laws, executive orders, and judicial decisions that have been generated over the years are unconstitutional for when those laws, executive orders and judicial decisions are critically and rigorously examined, they usually are not capable of passing the litmus test entailed by the guarantee of republican government.

Furthermore, this means that many of the decisions and practices of: Congress, the Executive Office, and the Judiciary that are cited as precedent to support or rationalize their judgments actually often constitute invalid forms of reasoning. This is so because such precedents are frequently the result of processes that could not satisfy the guarantee of republican government that is stipulated in Article IV, Section 4 of the Constitution and that all governmental officials are required by Constitutional authority to support through affirmation or oath ... as is said in another context, such precedents are the fruit of a poisonous tree (the failure to satisfy the conditions of republican government) and, as such, are, therefore, Constitutionally unacceptable.

To name just a few of the fruits of such a poisonous tree, one might mention: The Federal Reserve Act of 1913. The entire Act was put together in a secret meeting on Jekyll Island, off the coast of Georgia, by a group of seven individuals (Charles, Norton, Paul Warburg, Nelson Aldrich, Benjamin Strong, Abraham Andrew, Henry Davidson, and Frank Vanderlip) who represented a variety of private banking and financial interests and, then the Act was guided through Congress by people (such as Nelson Aldrich, who was the Republican Whip for the Senate) and who knew that the proposed Federal Reserve would not be a Federal institution but a corporation that served the interests of a consortium of private member banks rather than the interests of the vast majority of the people of the United States and that, for the most part, would be beyond the control of the Federal or State governments.

The foregoing was a clear violation of the guarantee of republican government. This is so not only in relation to the influence that special interests had in constructing the legislation concerning the Federal Reserve (and, there are many, many cases in which private lobbyists and special interest groups write the legislation that is voted on – often unknowingly -- by members of Congress), but the failure to observe the requirements of republican governance also reflects how many people in Congress failed to exercise reasonableness, integrity, honor, impartiality, honesty, judiciousness, impartiality, and benevolence (to anyone but the bankers) during the process of passing the Federal Reserve Act.

In fact, much of the legislation that deregulated the financial industry – e.g., the Glass-Steagall Act of 1933 – and which laid the groundwork for the creation of intentionally complex and mystifying financial instruments, such as derivatives, is unconstitutional. This is because the manner through which many, if not most, of the deregulatory laws came into existence violated the peoples' right to republican governance ... that is, many individuals who were involved with the passage of such legislation were not people with: honor, integrity, honesty, judiciousness, benevolence, impartiality, egalitarianism, independence, and high-mindedness that was free of all self-interest and private passions concerning such legislation.

Another example of the fruit of the poisonous tree concerns corporations. In today's world, corporations possess great power, have most of the rights and protections of actual human beings, and, yet rather ironically, often don't have any of the responsibilities of biological persons.

This current state of affairs has turned the understanding and concerns of colonists and the Framers of the Constitution upside down. In colonial days, corporations were, for the most part, loathed by the colonists – except, of course, for those individuals who stood to gain money and power through their cohabitation with one of the predominant corporations of colonial days – namely, the East India Company.

The Boston Tea Party was an act of rebellion not only against King George, but it was also a statement of protest against the East India Company that had been given an unfair advantage in commerce by being largely exempt from the taxes that were being levied on colonial tea entrepreneurs through the Tea Act of 1773. The East India Company, that had English government office holders and royalty among its stockholders, used the leverage provided to it through the Tea Act to drive smaller tea suppliers out of business by undercutting the prices charged by the latter who had to pay a tax from which the East India Company was largely immune.

The Framers of the Constitution had no intention of, either explicitly or implicitly, delegating rights and powers to corporations. Corporations are not mentioned in the main body of the Constitution nor in any of the amendments for a very good reason – corporations were considered to be malevolent forces intent on denying people the right to have control over their own lives.

However, despite the provisions of the Constitution, corporations have continued to seek ways to undermine democracy and usurp the powers of: the people, states, and the federal government. They have sought to accomplish this through a variety of venues, many of which involved the corporations who owned railroads.

For instance, consider the 1886 Supreme Court decision involving Santa Clara County versus Santa Fe Railroad. Over the years since that decision, corporations have tried to use what they have incorrectly portrayed as the substantive character of that decision as a precedent for treating corporations as persons. However, the attempt of corporations to push for such recognition violates the essential spirit of what is meant by republican governance in several ways.

First, the Santa Clara County decision did not acknowledge or stipulate that corporations were persons. Instead, the impression that such a precedent had been established was created by a court reporter – J.C. Bancroft Davis, a former executive for the railroads, and who, while employed as a court reported for the Supreme Court, earned money on the side by publishing Supreme Court decision with annotated introductions of his own thoughts. It was those annotated comments of the court reporter – not the actual legal decision -- which made the claim that the aforementioned decision had stipulated that corporations were persons under the law.

Secondly, the idea that: corporations were persons under the law and, therefore, were entitled to the same rights or powers as biological persons, would have been rejected by the vast majority of colonists as well as by the Framers of the Constitution. To try to argue otherwise would require one to rewrite America's revolutionary history, and, as a result, one has no problem in ascertaining the Framers' intent in relation to corporations like The East India Company – such corporations were predatory capitalists and to whatever extent they were permitted to exist, they should not be given any powers or rights that could not be completely controlled or revoked by the people.

Since then, corporations have used money, economic power and collusion with their corporate partners, the banks, to corrupt the political process in America and everywhere else in the world. Consequently, all of the powers and rights that corporations have acquired through the process of government have been gained by ensuring that the guarantee of republican government is ignored and corrupted.

In fact, one can take the issue further. Any attempt to consider corporations as anything other than legal fictions with respect to the very circumscribed category of artificial persons in order to provide civil liability protection with respect to monetary debt or damages in relation to investors of such artificial entities cannot pass the litmus test concerning the Constitutional guarantee of republican government. Moreover, all attempts to claim 14th Amendment protection for corporations are also unconstitutional because the 14th Amendment clearly stipulates that its provisions are specifically for: "all persons born or naturalized in the United States" and corporations are neither born nor naturalized.

Indeed, corporations are not citizens at all – born or naturalized. Thus, when one reads a bit further down in the 14th Amendment that: "No state shall make or enforce any law that shall abridge the privileges or immunities of citizens of the United States", this does not prevent laws being made that do abridge any privileges or immunities that corporations might believe themselves to have – and this is so, because corporations are not citizens.

Finally, the last part of Section 1 of the 14th Amendment states that no state might: "deny to any person within its jurisdiction the equal protection of the laws." A corporation is not a person in the sense of a being who has come into this world through biological birth and is a citizen of the United States by either birth or a process of naturalization, and, therefore, corporations are not entitled to equal protection under the law.

The entire history of corporations seeking to be legally identified as actual persons or being recognized by certain jurists as actual persons is predicated on a failure to comply with the requirements of the guarantee of republican government. This is so because all such efforts have been rooted in desires and qualities that are the antithesis of the sort of republican values and principles that are alluded to in Article IV, Section 4 of the Constitution – in other words those efforts have not exhibited properties of: benevolence, disinterest in personal gain, being unbiased, honesty, virtuousness, having integrity, and not possessing self-interest or private passions.

One could extend the foregoing sort of reasoning to a wide variety of other issues. For instance, passage of the Patriot Act -- along with so many other Congressional Acts – is unconstitutional because most of the members of

Congress did not read the Act before passing it. This is a violation of the guarantee of republican government.

One could add other examples of violations of the Constitutional guarantee of republican government. Conflicts involving Vietnam, Panama, Grenada, Nicaragua, Iraq (twice), and Afghanistan were -- and are -- unconstitutional ... irrespective of what Congress, the Executive Office, or the Judiciary claims. All those conflicts involved demonstrable: deceit, dishonesty, injudiciousness, unreasonableness, bias, and, as well, all those conflicts lacked: character, honorableness, integrity, benevolence, and impartiality. Consequently, all of those conflicts have failed to comply with the Constitutional guarantee of republican government that the federal government owes to the states.

The requirement of republican government is the lens through which all issues of national security and interests must be assessed. No war can be declared and no conflict can be fought unless one can demonstrate that the war and the conflict comply with republican principles and values.

Moreover, if, either after the fact or before the fact, a given war or conflict can be shown to be based, or to have been based, on lies (as say, Vietnam, Iraq – twice -- and Afghanistan have been so exposed), then the perpetrators of such essential breeches of the Constitution need to be impeached, if still in office, convicted, and then, whether, or not they hold elective or appointive office, held accountable for having committed: war crimes, crimes against humanity, and treason in relation to the very principles and purposes for which America came into being.

Or, consider the following. All government treaties and policies involving Native Peoples have been unconstitutional because they all violated, in one way or another, the Constitutional guarantee of republican government to the states and their people.

Nothing that the federal government has done in relation to Native peoples can be characterized as being: honorable, reasonable, impartial, unbiased, honest, tolerant, virtuous, benevolent, or disinterested. Throughout its history, the Federal Government has consistently and continuously violated Article IV, Section 4 of the Constitution by failing to provide citizens of the various states with republican governance in relation to a proper treatment of Native Peoples – some of whom provided ideas that helped shape and orient the thinking of the Framers of the Constitution.

Every rider that is added to a Congressional Bill – riders that seek some sort of special entitlement for a given state, district, region, or group as an implicit price for passing the bill in question -- is a violation of Article IV, Section of the Constitution. The very existence of such riders is demonstrated proof that the Bill to which they are attached lacks: integrity, independence, impartiality, honor, character, honesty, judiciousness, and virtuousness.

This might be how Congress operates. However, to the extent that this is the way Congress operates, then all such activities are unconstitutional since they are a violation of the guarantee of republican governance that is owed to the citizens of all the states in America.

Furthermore, many of the laws encompassing: elections, the unfair advantage that the Republican and Democratic Parties have in most jurisdictions, the way in which votes are recorded in many places (e.g., the newer electronic devices that leave no paper trail to verify the integrity of the process), campaign financing, and the use of public airwaves in relation to candidate debates and coverage are in violation of the Constitutional guarantee of republican government for all citizens of the respective states. This means that the elections arising out of such processes are also unconstitutional, for the latter are functionally related to the former activities – activities that lack often lack: integrity, honor, equitability, judiciousness, impartiality, egalitarianism, virtuousness, and character.

How the legislation is worded, or what might be said by various jurists in their decisions concerning this, or that, precedent in any of the foregoing matters, is often irrelevant. This is because the process through which the legislation has been generated or the judicial decisions that have been reached concerning such legislation give expression to numerous violations of the guarantee of republican governance.

Thus, even if one wanted to argue that Congress had constitutional authority to pass a law through which the 9/11 Commission was created (which I do not believe they had and will argue as much shortly), and even if one wished to maintain (which I do not believe can be done in a plausible way … again, more on this shortly) that the Department of Commerce had constitutional authority to direct NIST to undertake a series of reports concerning the collapse of the three buildings at the World Trade Center (although one might wonder why their alleged mandate did not include the Pentagon as well), there is a wealth of evidence to indicate that neither Congress, nor the 9/11 Commission, nor NIST, nor the Pentagon conducted themselves in accordance with the specifications of Article IV, Section 4 of the Constitution which stipulates that the Federal Government is under Constitutional obligation to guarantee republican government for all of the states and their respective peoples in such matters. Indeed, a litany of questions and charges (that I won't reiterate here and might easily be found in a variety of references) have been raised concerning the: honesty, integrity, independence, judiciousness, character, virtuousness, impartiality, reasonableness, and disinterestedness of: Congress, the 9/11 Commission, NIST, and the

Pentagon in relation to their respective investigations into 9/11.

In other words, neither Congress, nor the 9/11 Commission, nor NIST, nor the Pentagon, nor the Office of the President, nor the judiciary have met the litmus test of republican government in relation to 9/11. This is not a matter of officials making promises and, then, not living up to them, but, instead, this is a matter of all branches of the Federal Government having failed to meet the conditions of Article IV, Section 4 of the Constitution that guarantees a republican form of government in all matters.

Guarantees are not about giving a good faith effort – and, even this is questionable concerning the way the Federal Government handled the events prior to, on, and following 9/11. Guarantees are about the absolute fiduciary responsibility of all branches of government to ensure that republican values are instituted in everything that is done by any of those branches of government.

There is only one place in the Constitution in which any guarantees are given. This concerns the manner in which all activity – no matter which branch -- of the Federal Government must be conform to the principles, values, and spirit of republican governance.

There are no exceptions to Article IV, Section 4. This is the very heart of the Constitution, and if that provision is disregarded, then, all ensuing governance will be corrupted and become corrupt due to the absence of republican principles and values.

All one has to do is look at the current situation in the United States politically, economically, socially, educationally, financially, militarily, judicially, and internationally and one can see the effects that have ensued as a result of the United States persistent and pervasive disregard in relation to the central importance of republican government to a constitutionally viable democracy. The Framers of the Constitution understood this issue, but most of us have written off the guarantee of republican government as a quaint artifact of ancient history, and, as a result, we are suffering the consequences.

The 9/11 Commission Report, the various NIST reports, as well as *The Pentagon Performance Report* were all conceived in, and dedicated to, the proposition that they did not have to comply with the requirements of Article IV, Section 4 of the Constitution. This was a continuation of the acts and policies that the federal government had begun perpetrating before, during, and after the events of 9/11.

As a result, we have been graced with such things as: torture, extreme rendition, militarism, imperialism, enemy combatants, military tribunals, destruction of foreign countries, financial meltdowns, economic exploitation, loss of civil liberties, corporate malevolence, increasingly unmanageable debt; a failing infrastructure,

Congressional gridlock, and the loss of hundreds of thousands of lives (including some that were our own). Irrespective of how one might feel about what might, or might not, have occurred on 9/11, the fact of the matter is that the Constitution has been eviscerated by a succession of federal administrations who have failed to keep faith with the Framers' guarantee of republican government for the citizens of all the states in America.

-----

(2), (3) and (4).

All of the Framers of the Constitution, along with most of the colonists, believed that rights were extra-governmental. In other words, rights were inherent in their status as human beings and were not derived from, or gifts bestowed by, government.

The foregoing belief is given unmistakable expression in the second paragraph of the Declaration of Independence. Indeed, the idea of democratic government presupposed the existence of human beings who had the sort of naturally endowed rights that would enable them to come together and fashion a form of governance that would protect those rights within a framework that would help advance the common welfare along with all of the other principles mentioned in the Preamble to the Constitution.

Article I, Section 1 of the Constitution stipulates that" "All legislative powers herein granted shall be vested in the Congress of the United States, which shall consist of a Senate and a House of Representative." The legislative powers that are alluded to in Article I, Section 1 are specified in Section 8 of the same Article.

More specifically, in Section 8 of Article I of the Constitution one notes the following enumerated powers to which Congress is entitled. These powers include the ability to: (a) collect and lay taxes; (b) borrow money; (c) regulate commerce; (d) establish conditions for naturalization and bankruptcy; (e) coin and regulate the value of money; (f) provide for the punishment of counterfeiting; (g) establish post offices; (h) promote science and useful arts through copyright protections; (i) constitute tribunals inferior to the Supreme Court; (j) define and punish crimes committed on the high seas; (k) declare war; (l) raise and support armies; (m) provide and maintain an army; (n) make rules for the government and regulation of the land and naval forces; (o) provide for calling forth the militia to execute the laws of the union, suppress insurrections, and repel invasions; (p) provide for organizing, arming, and disciplining the militia; ; (q) exercise exclusive legislation in relation to the District of Columbia and all places purchased by the consent of the legislature of the various states for erection of forts; magazines, arsenals, dockyards, and other needful buildings; and (r) make all laws that shall be necessary and proper for the carrying into execution the foregoing powers by this Constitution in the government of the United States, or in any department or officer thereof.

271

The foregoing powers are not absolute. They are constrained by: the Preamble to the Constitution and the guarantee of republican government.

In other words, powers cannot be executed in just any way Congress wishes. Those powers must be exercised in accordance with republican principles – which are guaranteed – and must be done to further the purposes set forth in the Preamble to the Constitution ... namely, "to form a more perfect union; establish justice; insure domestic tranquility; provide for the common defense; promote the general welfare, and secure the blessings of liberty to ourselves and our posterity."

Furthermore, the Preamble is not a piece of rhetorical fluff. Without it, the Constitution has no direction or purpose.

Just as the guarantee of republican government gives expression to how government is to conduct itself, so too, the Preamble touches on why pursuing a union of people through government is important and what government is supposed to accomplish.

Unfortunately, there is a great deal that goes on in the three branches of the Federal Government that does not serve the purposes for which the

Constitution was created. If one took almost any piece of legislation, executive order, or judicial decision and asked for a rigorous defense be given as to how such legislation, orders, or decisions advanced the causes of the Preamble to the Constitution, much of the former could be shown to be: arbitrary; problematic; inconsistent; unnecessary; ill-conceived; biased; ineffective; and injurious to justice, domestic tranquility, the common defense; the general welfare, and securing liberty for ourselves and posterity.

To the extent that the foregoing claim is true, then all legislation, executive orders, and judicial decisions that cannot be shown to be able to rigorously and demonstrably further the purposes of the Preamble really are unconstitutional. If one's legislation, orders and decisions cannot be shown to serve the purposes for which the Constitution was created, then, such legislation, orders and decisions are really antithetical to why the Constitution was originally created.

For instance, one might ask: How did the Congressional law that formed the 9/11 Commission advance the purposes inherent in the Preamble to the Constitution?

Did the 9/11 Commission help "form a more perfect union"? No, it didn't. The Commission and its executive director were riddled with conflicts of interest, and such conflicts of interest are an anathema to the idea of forming a more perfect union. Furthermore, *The 9/11 Commission Report* is also riddled with errors of many different kinds encompassing problems of both omission and commission, and, once again, it is very difficult, if not impossible, to understand how error is ever going to lead to the formation of a more perfect union.

273

Did the 9/11 Commission establish justice? No, it didn't because the Commissioners, researchers, and executive director went out of their ways not to establish justice except through statements, arguments, and inferences that were lacking evidential credibility and intent on promoting a conspiracy theory favored by the government. In fact, a terrible injustice was perpetrated on the 9/11 families, the American people, and the rest of the world through the 9/11 Commission and its report.

Did the Commission insure domestic tranquility? No, it didn't, and in fact it had exactly the opposite effect since a number of polls now indicate that well over a hundred and twenty million people (including a number of 9/11 families, as well as an array of professional pilots, architects, engineers, ex-military and intelligence offices, and scientists) in the United States now believe that the 9/11 Commission did not do a credible job in relation to its investigation of 9/11.

Did the Commission provide for the common defense? No, it didn't since it actually undermined the possibility of such a common defense through its many errors of commission (e.g., the

Commission intentionally left out the testimony of scores of people who had evidence that ran contrary to the government's conspiracy theory) and, as a result, made certain that many truths about 9/11 would never see the light of day – and, you cannot provide for the common defense by hiding the truth.

Did the Commission promote the general welfare? No, it didn't because the Commission was a body that was engaged in something other than a thorough and rigorous search for the truth -- which is the only thing that could have promoted the general welfare under the circumstances. Instead, America, 9/11 families, and the rest of the world have been fed a steady diet of misinformation, disinformation, and an invented mythology by *The 9/11 Commission Report.*

Did the Commission secure the blessings of liberty for either: ourselves or our posterity? No, it didn't but, instead, the Commission placed our liberties at risk through promoting and propagandizing a conspiracy theory that the government had advanced, without credible evidence, within days following the events of 9/11 – a conspiracy theory that *The 9/11th Commission Report* could not defensibly or plausibly maintain and, yet, a conspiracy theory that has been used by all too many people who should have known better to help rationalize and justify the dismantling of civil liberties in America, Iraq, and Afghanistan.

Since the 9/11 Commission, its researchers, its executive director, and its report were not advancing the principles of the Preamble to the Constitution, then they must have been advancing some other agenda. In other words, whatever was going on with the 9/11 Commission was unconstitutional.

In addition to the constraints imposed on Congressional legislative power by the Preamble to the Constitution and the guarantee of republican government, there are several amendments to the Constitution that are intended to remind everyone – government and citizens alike – that Congress is not entitled to extend its activities beyond the limits that are specified in the Constitution – almost all of which are contained in Section 8 of Article I and that have been outlined earlier. These two amendments are the ninth and tenth amendments.

Colonists, in general, as well as many of the people who were most active in the constitutional and ratification processes, in particular, were concerned that the federal government might try to extend its authority beyond the enumerated powers of Article I, Section 1 in the proposed Constitution. Therefore, they insisted that the Constitution be amended to reflect such a concern -- namely: "The enumeration in the Constitution of certain rights shall not be construed to deny or disparage others retained by the people," and this is known as the Ninth Amendment.

This meant that the powers and rights of Congress were fixed and limited by the Constitution. Moreover, whatever those powers were, they could not be extended in such a way as to deny or disparage the rights and powers that people retained beyond the enumerated powers and rights of Congress.

The protections of the Ninth Amendment were further strengthened through the Tenth Amendment. This amendment states that: "The powers not delegated to the United States, nor prohibited by it to the states, are reserved to the states, or to the people."

The Tenth Amendment accomplished two things. First, it reiterated an important principle, initially introduced through the Ninth Amendment – namely, citizens or the people have constitutional standing quite independently of the federal government or state governments.

If this were not the case, then the Ninth Amendment would have talked about how the enumeration of rights or powers belonging to the federal government should not be understood to either deny or disparage other rights and powers retained by the states. However, the Ninth Amendment did not mention state rights or powers. The amendment only referred to the rights and powers of the people.

Moreover, the Tenth Amendment affirms that the constitutional standing of people or citizens is independent of the federal governments when it

276

adds the phrase: "or to the people." If the Framers of the Constitution had wanted to reserve all powers for the states that have not been delegated to the federal government or that have not been prohibited to the state governments, then the Tenth Amendment would have ended with the words: "are reserved for the states," but this is not what the Tenth Amendment says.

When the issues underlying the Tenth Amendment were being discussed, Roger Sherman from Connecticut suggested that the phrase "or to the people" be added to the wording of the amendment. This suggestion was accepted without objection or debate.

One cannot read the Tenth Amendment as if the phrase: "or to the people," is just a literary device that offers another way of referring to state governments. Constitutionally speaking, state governments are one thing, and the people are quite another.

There was much suspicion among colonists concerning any kind of government, and this was a direct result of their collective experiences either in Europe and/or through the tyrannical manner in which the British (and their colonialist agents) sought to control things in America. This meant that not only was the idea of a central, federal government to be approached with caution and with respect to which citizens should have protections and relief, but the aforementioned suspicions concerning governance extended to both state and local governments as well.

The Bill of Rights is almost entirely dedicated to protections of people and not of states. The Tenth Amendment does offer protection to states, but, simultaneously, that amendment also extends protection to the people by clearly indicating that: people were to have constitutional standing alongside of states and that citizens had a choice as to whether they wished those powers that were not delegated to the federal government or prohibited to the states to fall within the purview of the people or the purview of state governments that, theoretically, represented citizens.

The people insisted on a Bill of Rights because they did not trust government – any government. The people insisted on the Ninth and Tenth Amendments because those amendments gave the people a constitutional standing that neither the federal government nor the state governments should deny or disparage.

Unfortunately, states historically have continuously sought to usurp the rights and powers of people that were granted to people under the Ninth and Tenth Amendments. States, in this respect, have tried to do to the people what the federal government has attempted to do in relation to the states and the people – that is, to extend the sphere power, influence, and control of the central government.

For example, let's return to the list of enumerated powers that are listed in Article I, Section 8 of the Constitution and that have been stated earlier. Nowhere in that list of powers is there anything indicating that Congress has the right and power to create legislation concerning a 9/11-kind of investigation.

The closest that the enumerated list comes to such a possibility is in relation to the power of tribunals. The primary root meaning of the idea of a tribunal is in the form of a court or forum of justice.

In fact, Article I, Section 8 indicates that the power at issue involves the capacity "to constitute tribunals inferior to the Supreme Court." This infuses the notion of tribunal with a thoroughly judicial flavor.

The 9/11 Commission did possess the power of subpoenas, and this is similar to what happens in relation to tribunals. Moreover, most witnesses had to swear an oath under possible penalty of perjury, and, again, this is somewhat similar to what occurs within tribunals.

Nonetheless, despite the foregoing surface similarities between the investigation of the 9/11 Commission and the idea of tribunal, the 9/11 Commission does not really satisfy most of the criteria that might justify calling such a process a tribunal. For instance: (1) the Commission was not constituted with a judicial purpose in mind but, from the beginning, was treated as an investigation; (2) there was no special prosecutor appointed; (3) there were no defendants; (4) there was no attempt to observe the laws of evidence or follow normal court procedure; (5) the entire process of research was kept hidden and was not subject to rules of disclosure or cross-examination; (6) there were witnesses (e.g. George W. Bush and Richard Cheney) who did not have to swear an oath before giving testimony; (7) no judge or judges were assigned to the investigation; (8) although there were witnesses who gave false testimony, no one was held accountable; (9) although the power of subpoena was available to the Commission, it was almost never used, and as a result, even if justice were the point of the exercise – which it wasn't – justice could never had been served by Commissioners who were, for whatever reason, unwilling to exercise the subpoena power in anything but a perfunctory and very limited manner; (10) there were no sanctions associated with the findings of the commission; (11) the findings of the 9/11 Commission were not subject to review by the Supreme Court that is clearly a requirement entailed by the Congressional power to be able to constitute tribunals that are "inferior to the Supreme Court".

One cannot try to claim that something is a tribunal when it ignores, or tramples upon, most of what a tribunal requires. Furthermore, even if one were to concede the idea that 9/11 Commission was a tribunal (which the foregoing points indicate is not the case), then, at the very best, such an individual is faced with the prospect that the 9/11 Commission was unconstitutional in the manner in which it violated the principles inherent in the Preamble to the Constitution, as well as unconstitutional in the way in which it violated the guarantee of republican government set forth in Article IV, Section of the Constitution.

The fact of the matter is, the 9/11 Commission was not a tribunal in: intent; name, form, principle, process, or results. Therefore, in passing legislation that created the 9/11 Commission, Congress exceeded its constitutional authority.

None of the powers that are enumerated in Article I, Section 8 of the Constitution entitle Congress to form a 9/11-style investigation. Congress could have created a tribunal that would have been required to pursue the issues surrounding 9/11 in a very different way than the 9/11 Commission did, but Congress didn't do this, and, therefore, the 9/11 Commission as constituted and realized was in violation of the Constitution.

According to the 9th Amendment, "the enumeration in the Constitution of certain rights shall not be construed to deny or disparage others retained by the people", and, yet, this is exactly what Congress did through the formation of the 9/11 Commission – deny and disparage rights that are retained by the people. According to the 10th Amendment, "the powers not delegated to the United States by the Constitution, nor prohibited to it by the states, are reserved to the states respectively, or to the people," and, yet, by passing legislation for the 9/11 Commission, Congress transgressed into areas that are clearly the preserve of, and reserved for, the states or the people.

By passing legislature to form the 9/11 Commission, Congress not only violated the 9th and 10th Amendment rights of the people as pointed out in the foregoing comments, but, as well, Congress violated the 5th Amendment rights of people. Among other things, the 5th Amendment introduces the idea of a "grand jury".

Normally speaking, grand juries are formed when a district attorney or attorney general wants to prosecute someone whom he or she believes has committed a crime. During the grand jury proceeding, the prosecutor puts forth an array of evidence that she or he believes strongly indicates that a given individual has committed a certain crime.

The members of the grand jury are free to ask whatever questions they like concerning such evidence. They also are free to ask for additional evidence and witnesses to be presented.

Once all the witnesses and evidence have been presented, the prosecutor leaves the room where the grand jury has been convened. The jurors then discuss and explore the issues among themselves as to whether, on not, they believe sufficient evidence has been presented to underwrite an indictment of the accused individual.

The understanding of many people – including that of some lawyers and prosecutors – concerning the idea of a grand jury tends to end at this point. In other words, once the grand jury reaches a decision concerning whether, or not, to indict someone, then supposedly the work of the grand jury is complete.

However, a grand jury does not serve the state or its legal officials. The grand jury serves the people, and the reason that the idea of a grand jury has been enshrined in the 5th Amendment is to preserve the civil liberties of citizens.

Consequently, on the one hand, grand juries are the last outpost of protection for citizens against arbitrary and unwarranted prosecution by the government. However, on the other hand, grand juries also are a constitutionally authorized forum to ensure that the government is not undermining the civil liberties of citizens in ways that might extend beyond the interests of any given district attorney, attorney general, or other legal representative of the government.

Once the immediate reasons for which some level of government has convened a grand jury have been served, a grand jury is free to pursue any other issue that is of interest to the members of that jury that carry implications for the civil liberties and rights of citizens. Many district attorneys and attorney generals who actually know about this dimension of the power of grand juries are often not inclined to share such knowledge with the members of a grand jury and, thereby, help those members understand the full potential of their power under the Constitution.

The powers of grand juries are entailed by the guarantee of a republican form of government for the states. The powers of grand juries are entailed by the rights inherent in the 9th and 10th Amendments – rights that belong to the people and not to the central government. The powers of grand juries are entailed by the principles given expression through the Preamble to the Constitution. The powers of grand juries are entailed by the priority that people have over governments through the natural, inborn rights of human beings and from which governments derive whatever authority they have.

By passing legislation that created the 9/11 Commission, Congress usurped the rights and powers of grand juries to make determinations and judgments in such matters. By passing legislation concerning 9/11, Congress attempted -- in contravention of the amended Constitution -- to deny and disparage the rights and powers of the people ... rights and powers that could be exercised through venues like, but not restricted to, a grand jury.

Furthermore, by participating in a commission that was without constitutional authority, each of the Commissioners, as well as the executive director of the Commission, and all of the Commission researchers did also effectively deprive the American people of the latter's 5th, 9th, and 10th Amendment rights. I do not call what the various participants did a conspiracy, but, rather, each person acted individually and, probably without any real understanding of the nature of their unconstitutional behavior. However, whether done unknowingly or knowingly, all those individuals were, nonetheless, still denying and depriving American citizens of their Constitutionally established rights by working with and on the 9/11 Commission.

Article II, Section 2 of the Constitution indicates that the President shall: "appoint ambassadors, other public ministers, and counsels, judges of the Supreme Court, and all other officers of the United States whose appointments are not herein otherwise provided for, and that shall be established by law." In conjunction with the 9/11 Commission, the President did appoint, first, Henry Kissinger, and, then, Thomas Kean to serve as Chairman of the 9/11 Commission.

However, the 9/11 Commission was created through Congressional legislation. It was not a Presidential body.

Thomas Kean was assigned to the Commission as the President's representative on a legislatively created body. As such, Thomas Kean had no special authority apart from what Congress had enabled (unconstitutionally) the Commission to have in the first place.

By appointing the chairman for the 9/11 Commission, the President violated the 5th, 9th, and

10th Amendment rights of the people because he was co-operating with a body – namely, the Congress – which had exceeded its Constitutional authority in relation to the powers that it had, and had not, been granted. Consequently, in the process, the President also exceeded his authority even though under other circumstances the President does have the Constitutional authority, as noted earlier, to appoint various individuals as ambassadors, Supreme Court judges, counsels, or officers of the United States.

In addition to Congress and the President, there is another facet of government that also violated the 5th, 9th, and 10th Amendment rights of the people. The facet of government to which allusion is being directed here concerns the Department of Commerce that authorized NIST (National Institute of Standards and Technology) to conduct an investigation into the building collapses at the World Trade Center.

NIST came into being in 1901 and is under the auspices of the Department of Commerce. It is a non-regulatory agency whose stated mission is: "to promote U.S. innovation and industrial competitiveness by advancing measurement science, standards, and technology in ways that enhance economic security and improve the quality of life."

Whatever technical facility NIST might have, neither the Department of Commerce nor NIST had Constitutional authority to investigate the World

Trade Center building collapses. The investigation of those collapses was not about, on the one hand, regulating commerce, nor, on the other hand, was such an investigation a matter of promoting innovation and industrial competitiveness, or advancing: measurement science, standards, and/or technology.

Even if one were to concede that the Department of Commerce and, therefore, NIST had Constitutional authority to conduct the investigation it did with respect to the World Trade Center (which I do not concede and that they cannot justify under the Constitution), overwhelming evidence exists through the work of people such as: Richard Gage, Steven Jones, Judy Wood, Kevin Ryan, and many, many others that NIST did not conduct itself in accordance with its Constitutionally mandated obligation to go about its activities in compliance with republican principles of: honesty; integrity; honor; impartiality; judiciousness; character; independence; or reasonableness.

Moreover, it seems rather odd that NIST was given authority to investigate the collapse of the World Trade buildings, rather than, say, the National Transportation Safety Board or the FBI. Of course, in many ways, neither the NTSB nor the FBI is really equipped with the resources and expertise to examine the collapse of three buildings at the World Trade Center except in very restricted ways.

Unfortunately, almost from the very beginning, the FBI failed to treat the World Trade Center as a crime scene. The FBI permitted evidence to be taken away without consideration for the possibility that its theory concerning the nature of events on 9/11 might be incorrect or incomplete, and, consequently, as an agency of the central government, the FBI violated the Constitutional guarantee of a republican form of government for the states – a possibility that assumes more ironic proportions given that the FBI has, since, publically stated they have absolutely no credible evidence capable of tying 'Usama bin Laden to the events of 9/11.

One might also add that the FBI has acted unconstitutionally in the manner in which it has handled potential evidence about 9/11 involving, among others, Sibel Edmonds, Indira Singh, Robert Wright, and David Schippers. In the first three cases, the FBI has put a gag order on the people in question and, as a result, has prevented those individuals from sharing what they know with the American people.

The provisions of Article IV, Section 4 of the Constitution are quite clear. The federal government – including all of its agencies – are under an absolute guarantee to provide a republican form of government to the states of the union, and, yet, based on what <u>has</u> been said by Edmonds, Singh, Wright, and Schippers, the FBI has not acted with: impartiality; honesty; honor;

integrity;   judiciousness;   character;   or reasonableness in relation to 9/11.

The cry of 'National Security' does not trump a constitutional guarantee of republican government. This is especially so when there is prima facie evidence provided by, at least, four individuals, acting independently of one another, that the FBI has not conducted itself in accordance with the Constitutional requirement of republican government with respect to the events of 9/11.

In addition, the mantra of "National Security" also does not justify the use of torture water-boarding, extreme rendition, the invention of categories such as "unlawful enemy combatant", or maintaining captives without due process. The military and all intelligence agencies are under the auspices of the federal government, and, therefore, they are subject to the requirements of Article IV, Section 4 concerning the guarantee of republican government to all states – and this remains true whether, or not, the country is at war or engaged in some military conflict.

If the federal government in any of its manifestations does not comply with the Constitutional guarantee of republican government, then national security has been violated because there is nothing more vital to the national security of America than the requirements of republican government. There is nothing more important or essential to Constitutional stability and viability than the requirement that all federal employees (whether members of Congress, members of the military, members of the so-called intelligence community, members of the judiciary, or members of any department or office within the federal government) act with: integrity, character, honesty, impartiality, judiciousness, benevolence, independence, honor, self-sacrifice (not the sacrifice of others), and virtue. Moreover, if federal employees cannot act in the foregoing manner, then everything they do is unconstitutional.

Currently, despite whatever successes and good features might be present, the United States is a failed state. It is a failed state because it gives expression to all the characteristics of a failed state.

More specifically:

(1) Failed States do not honor the provisions and guarantees of their constitutional documents – and the foregoing discussion has shown that the United States federal government has done this again and again.

(2) Failed states are unwilling or unable to protect their citizens – e.g., 9/11; Katrina; the BP/Deep Water Horizon catastrophe (along with many other environmental disasters); the financial meltdowns involving derivatives; the banking industry; endless wars for contrived reasons.

(3) Failed states tend to regard themselves as beyond the reach of domestic and international law

– e.g., America's opting out of the World Court, as well as its undermining the United Nations by continuing to support Israel's illegal occupation and confiscation of Palestinian property, as well as Israel's illegal: wall, settlements and violation of Palestinian human rights.

(4) Failed states feel free, if not entitled, to carry out aggression and violence against other countries and peoples – e.g., the United States' acts of unprovoked aggression against Iran, Guatemala, Cuba, Vietnam, Lebanon, Nicaragua, Chile, Grenada, Panama, Haiti, Iraq (twice), Afghanistan, Pakistan, and the Palestinian people.

(5) Failed states suffer from a deficit of democratic institutions – e.g., America's legal system Is broken and disadvantages the poor in all too many ways; congress is deadlocked and almost completely under the influence and control of lobbyists and special interests; the military is used as a tool for imperialistic and corporate agendas; the electoral process is deeply dysfunctional; the executive office often behaves as if it is a monarchical, imperial presidency that does not have to serve anything but its own agenda.

(6) Failed states usually have no, or little control, over their central banks or actively collude with such banks to the disadvantage of the vast majority of their citizens so that the latter are enslaved by the banking system rather than empowered by it – e.g., the Federal Reserve system is a consortium of private banking interests that

was unconstitutionally legislated into existence and has never once been able to avert any of the crises (such as the Great Depression or the current near-Depression and the recent meltdown in the financial markets) for which it, allegedly, was created.

292

(7) Failed states are characterized by a media whose behavior and potential for objectivity and integrity have, in many ways, been co-opted -- e.g., if the American media had been objective and acted with integrity in relation to the events of 9/11 – which they did not—then America's present situation might not be so dire.

(8) Failed states terrorize their own citizens and the citizens of other countries – e.g., the persistent evisceration of the American Constitution that has been perpetrated by all three branches of the federal government over the last several hundred years is nothing less than a series of terrorist attacks upon successive generations of American citizens, and such terrorist attacks have permitted other terrorist activities by the federal government to spill over into America's treatment of many other countries and peoples around the world.

In view of the foregoing, I believe that there are roughly five choices facing the American people:

(a) Acknowledge that the 9/11 Commission was an unconstitutional usurpation of the rights of citizens under the 5th, 9th and 10th Amendments of the Constitution, as well as a violation of both the

Preamble to the Constitution and Article IV, Section 4 of the Constitution that guarantees republican government to all of the sates of the union, and, as a result, permit American citizens – not the government – to pursue a new investigation into the events: leading up to, occurring on, and ensuing from 9/11. This could be a first, and very necessary step that permits Americans to reclaim and reassert their right to a constitutional democracy that has integrity and other qualities of republican governance.

(b) Convene a new Constitutional convention in which the American people have an opportunity to correct all the things that currently help make the United States a failed nation.

(c) Permit states to secede and make their own arrangements – alone or in concert -- and I might point out that although I consider much of the recent discussions concerning secession by various states (e.g., Texas) to be of a frivolous and ill-conceived nature, states do have the right to secede from the Union if the federal government breaks the Constitutional contract that binds states together. In fact, secession is one of the rights and powers that is entailed by the 9th and 10th Amendments, and, therefore, Lincoln was wrong when he sought to force states to remain in the Union. However poorly conceived a move to secede might be, it is neither necessarily an act of insurrection, nor is it an act of sedition or treason, and, therefore, the federal government has no power to prevent it. When the federal government, or any of its agents, no longer complies with the requirements of republican government, then the federal government has lent justification to the desire that people or states might carry with respect to the issue of secession.

(d) Enter into a series of bloody, chaotic rebellions, insurgencies, and insurrections through which multiple parties all vie to control other human beings and deprive the latter of their natural, inherent rights as human beings.

(e) Go with the status quo and be sucked down by the whirlpool in the toilet of an increasingly failed state.

The first option noted above – that is, holding a new, rigorous, independent investigation into the events surrounding 9/11-- is the easiest and least problematic choice facing the American people. Moreover, pursuing that choice might be the best chance America has of pulling back from the precipice of destruction on which the country is teetering.

The second option – that is, convening a new constitutional convention – might serve as a very constructive complement to the foregoing option. Although there is a great deal about America that is right, there also is far too much about America that is dysfunctional and destructive (with respect to ourselves and others), and, therefore, there is a deep need to revitalize and rededicate our democracy through establishing methods and principles that might permit America to be better than it has been over the last several hundred years.

Although the last three options noted above are actual possibilities that are staring us in the face, I don't see any of them as being able to constructively solve the problems with which Americans are currently confronted even as I see different groups within the general population who seem to be increasingly advocating some form of secession, insurrection, or rebellion. Moreover, I feel that those individuals who believe that America will somehow stumble through the current Constitutional crisis without being required to change, in any essential way, the nature of governance or without having to change what is currently going on within government, are suffering from a form of thinking that is seriously delusional in nature.

We can choose to rid ourselves of our current failed state status, and I believe the first step in this process involves either: initiating a new, citizen-controlled but constitutionally authorized investigation into 9/11, and/or convening a new Constitutional convention. The alternative to the foregoing is that we can choose to become an increasingly failed state through secession, insurrection, rebellion, or maintaining the status quo.

America is at a tipping point. The fracture lines are running in all directions, and although just as no one can predict when a major earthquake will occur, all the indices are present to point to a coming cataclysmic social and political event or series of such events in our collective futures.

Time is running out. Important choices need to be made now, or very soon the capacity to choose might be ripped from our hands by social, political, and economic events that could inundate us in an irreversible fashion.